HowExpe~~rt Guide~~ to Mont~~pelier,~~ Vermont

101+ Tips to Learn the History, Discover the Best Places to Visit, Find Fun Things to Do, and Enjoy the Smallest Capital in the USA

HowExpert with Jody Andreoletti

Copyright HowExpert™
www.HowExpert.com

For more tips related to this topic, visit HowExpert.com/montpelier.

Recommended Resources

- HowExpert.com – How To Guides on All Topics from A to Z by Everyday Experts.
- HowExpert.com/free – Free HowExpert Email Newsletter.
- HowExpert.com/books – HowExpert Books
- HowExpert.com/courses – HowExpert Courses
- HowExpert.com/clothing – HowExpert Clothing
- HowExpert.com/membership – HowExpert Membership Site
- HowExpert.com/affiliates – HowExpert Affiliate Program
- HowExpert.com/jobs – HowExpert Jobs
- HowExpert.com/writers – Write About Your #1 Passion/Knowledge/Expertise & Become a HowExpert Author.
- HowExpert.com/resources – Additional HowExpert Recommended Resources
- YouTube.com/HowExpert – Subscribe to HowExpert YouTube.
- Instagram.com/HowExpert – Follow HowExpert on Instagram.
- Facebook.com/HowExpert – Follow HowExpert on Facebook.
- TikTok.com/@HowExpert – Follow HowExpert on TikTok.

Publisher's Foreword

Dear HowExpert Reader,

HowExpert publishes quick 'how to' guides on all topics from A to Z by everyday experts.

At HowExpert, our mission is to discover, empower, and maximize everyday people's talents to ultimately make a positive impact in the world for all topics from A to Z...one everyday expert at a time!

All of our HowExpert guides are written by everyday people just like you and me, who have a passion, knowledge, and expertise for a specific topic.

We take great pride in selecting everyday experts who have a passion, real-life experience in a topic, and excellent writing skills to teach you about the topic you are also passionate about and eager to learn.

We hope you get a lot of value from our HowExpert guides, and it can make a positive impact on your life in some way. All of our readers, including you, help us continue living our mission of positively impacting the world for all spheres of influences from A to Z.

If you enjoyed one of our HowExpert guides, then please take a moment to send us your feedback from wherever you got this book.

Thank you, and we wish you all the best in all aspects of life.

Sincerely,

BJ Min
Founder & Publisher of HowExpert
HowExpert.com

PS...If you are also interested in becoming a HowExpert author, then please visit our website at HowExpert.com/writers. Thank you & again, all the best!

COPYRIGHT, LEGAL NOTICE AND DISCLAIMER:

COPYRIGHT © BY HOT METHODS, INC. (DBA HOWEXPERT™). ALL RIGHTS RESERVED WORLDWIDE. NO PART OF THIS PUBLICATION MAY BE REPRODUCED IN ANY FORM OR BY ANY MEANS, INCLUDING SCANNING, PHOTOCOPYING, OR OTHERWISE WITHOUT PRIOR WRITTEN PERMISSION OF THE COPYRIGHT HOLDER.

DISCLAIMER AND TERMS OF USE: PLEASE NOTE THAT MUCH OF THIS PUBLICATION IS BASED ON PERSONAL EXPERIENCE AND ANECDOTAL EVIDENCE. ALTHOUGH THE AUTHOR AND PUBLISHER HAVE MADE EVERY REASONABLE ATTEMPT TO ACHIEVE COMPLETE ACCURACY OF THE CONTENT IN THIS GUIDE, THEY ASSUME NO RESPONSIBILITY FOR ERRORS OR OMISSIONS. ALSO, YOU SHOULD USE THIS INFORMATION AS YOU SEE FIT, AND AT YOUR OWN RISK. YOUR PARTICULAR SITUATION MAY NOT BE EXACTLY SUITED TO THE EXAMPLES ILLUSTRATED HERE; IN FACT, IT'S LIKELY THAT THEY WON'T BE THE SAME, AND YOU SHOULD ADJUST YOUR USE OF THE INFORMATION AND RECOMMENDATIONS ACCORDINGLY.

THE AUTHOR AND PUBLISHER DO NOT WARRANT THE PERFORMANCE, EFFECTIVENESS OR APPLICABILITY OF ANY SITES LISTED OR LINKED TO IN THIS BOOK. ALL LINKS ARE FOR INFORMATION PURPOSES ONLY AND ARE NOT WARRANTED FOR CONTENT, ACCURACY OR ANY OTHER IMPLIED OR EXPLICIT PURPOSE.

ANY TRADEMARKS, SERVICE MARKS, PRODUCT NAMES OR NAMED FEATURES ARE ASSUMED TO BE THE PROPERTY OF THEIR RESPECTIVE OWNERS, AND ARE USED ONLY FOR REFERENCE. THERE IS NO IMPLIED ENDORSEMENT IF WE USE ONE OF THESE TERMS.

NO PART OF THIS BOOK MAY BE REPRODUCED, STORED IN A RETRIEVAL SYSTEM, OR TRANSMITTED BY ANY OTHER MEANS: ELECTRONIC, MECHANICAL, PHOTOCOPYING, RECORDING, OR OTHERWISE, WITHOUT THE PRIOR WRITTEN PERMISSION OF THE AUTHOR.

ANY VIOLATION BY STEALING THIS BOOK OR DOWNLOADING OR SHARING IT ILLEGALLY WILL BE PROSECUTED BY LAWYERS TO THE FULLEST EXTENT. THIS PUBLICATION IS PROTECTED UNDER THE US COPYRIGHT ACT OF 1976 AND ALL OTHER APPLICABLE INTERNATIONAL, FEDERAL, STATE AND LOCAL LAWS AND ALL RIGHTS ARE RESERVED, INCLUDING RESALE RIGHTS: YOU ARE NOT ALLOWED TO GIVE OR SELL THIS GUIDE TO ANYONE ELSE.

THIS PUBLICATION IS DESIGNED TO PROVIDE ACCURATE AND AUTHORITATIVE INFORMATION WITH REGARD TO THE SUBJECT MATTER COVERED. IT IS SOLD WITH THE UNDERSTANDING THAT THE AUTHORS AND PUBLISHERS ARE NOT ENGAGED IN RENDERING LEGAL, FINANCIAL, OR OTHER PROFESSIONAL ADVICE. LAWS AND PRACTICES OFTEN VARY FROM STATE TO STATE AND IF LEGAL OR OTHER EXPERT ASSISTANCE IS REQUIRED, THE SERVICES OF A PROFESSIONAL SHOULD BE SOUGHT. THE AUTHORS AND PUBLISHER SPECIFICALLY DISCLAIM ANY LIABILITY THAT IS INCURRED FROM THE USE OR APPLICATION OF THE CONTENTS OF THIS BOOK.

COPYRIGHT BY HOT METHODS, INC. (DBA HOWEXPERT™)
ALL RIGHTS RESERVED WORLDWIDE.

Table of Contents

Chapter 1 How to Get the Most Out Of the Smallest Capital in the United States

1.1 Overview

Montpelier, Vermont, boasts a population of just over 7,000 residents, which makes it the most small-town capital city in the country. It also makes Montpelier the easiest capital city in the country to absorb, enjoy, and immerse yourself in because you can focus your energy on just a few square miles of condensed interests and events. Instead of walking blocks or miles to get from one destination to the next, your next stop is usually quite close by. It doesn't matter really what you want to see here; it's all about a block away from where you are. Just kidding. Sometimes it's not even that far.

Montpelier has a rich history of ingenuity, manufacturing, war-relief efforts, and political progress, which this book will tell you all about as you read on. You won't find any McDonald's, Starbucks, or really much of any big franchise businesses outside of gas stations. Montpelier is all about embracing the local economy, which in turn supports many of our neighbors whom we want to see succeed. We are very proud of our town, and we want you to feel the same warm energy we live in every day. What follows in this chapter are some high-level tips so that when you arrive, you are ready to fully experience what this tiny capital has to offer.

1.2 Taking in the town

1.2.1 Downtown

The major draw when you first get here is the downtown area, which includes the State House building. It's hard to miss because of its gleaming golden dome, which, by the way, is painted with 24-carat gold leaf and has been regilded about ten times since the first application in 1906. When I was a kid, the rumor was that if you scraped all of the gold on, it would fit into a small ball in your hand, and that is, in fact, true. The gold leaf used on the dome is enough to make about a half bar of gold.

State Street and Main Street are the two major thoroughfares through town, and you can easily find your way to State Street when you get off the highway because the Capitol building can be seen as you drive in. Most of our local shops and restaurants are situated on State and Main, with a few located on smaller streets just off the main ones.

Almost everything in the downtown area is within walking distance, and most of it is flat terrain. That's the magic of small New England towns: they are often in the valley between mountains or hills. But if you start walking down a hill to get somewhere, be aware you will have to walk back up! Conversely, "what goes up, must come down" will work to your advantage when you hike in Hubbard Park or walk to Vermont College.

Tip 1: Find the State & Main intersection.

This one lighted intersection in the middle of town is a good starting point for all adventuring. Not only is it easy to find, but it also offers some great "small town" photos of shop-lined streets and seasonally-dressed passers-by. It's especially beautiful after a fresh snow, where the lights, trees, buildings, and cars are covered in white. Add in a few well-layered pedestrians in their boots and hats, and you've got a Norman Rockwell painting waiting to happen.

Tip 2: Stay overnight in town.

The best way to fully enjoy the town is to stay overnight so you can park your car and walk everywhere. Of course, there are cheaper hotels further outside of town, and if that's what your budget affords, you will still enjoy your time when you come to Montpelier. Still, if you can spring for one of our local hotels or inns, it is worth it for the comfort and immersion into small-town living.

The Capitol Plaza, for example, is a plush hotel on State Street, right in the middle of everything. They serve breakfast, lunch, and dinner at their in-house restaurant, J. Morgan's.

Tip 3: Bring the kids to see the miniature trains running through the restaurant!

The owner of the hotel has always enjoyed model trains, and even though the restaurant has been remodeled, it kept the model trains running on tracks high on the walls. It's a great distraction for kids while you wait for your meal.

If you time your stay around Mother's Day, you can visit their extravagant Mother's Day buffet that fills an entire conference room with tables of salads, hors d'oeuvres, vegetables, sandwiches, pastas, and desserts, as well as their brilliant omelet, waffle, and carving stations.

If you want to level up your accommodations, you can book a room at The Inn at Montpelier. Well-kept, ornate architecture inside and out, they also offer casual yet classy dining at The Social and on their wrap-around porch in the fairer months. This was also the location of my first job when I was 16, working as a back waiter in the upscale dining room. Besides serving tea, coffee, and desserts on silver trays, I used to sprint through the low ceilings of their extensive wine cellar basement to locate bottles of expensive vino and then rush back upstairs and pretend that I wasn't out of breath when I was back in the public eye. Total professional here.

1.2.2 Neighborhoods

Many of our historic neighborhoods are woven into the downtown area or rest just outside. If you are only going to be in town for a day, it's a great idea to take a quick car trip around them to see the many examples of Victorian, Second Empire French, and Queen Anne architecture that denote the earlier days of Montpelier. Amongst some of the modern construction, you will find homes dating back to the early 1800s and 1900s. There is even a private home that was originally a Civil War arsenal.

1.2.3 Outdoor Recreation

Winter feels like a very long season here, so to adapt, we find many ways to get outside throughout the year, especially when it's cold. A lot of the outdoor spaces in town are creatively used for multiple purposes, so they can be uniquely fun during any season. Grassy hills at schools, parks, or homes become sliding hills in the winter. Swimming holes become skating ponds. Running trails become cross-country skiing trails. Even the State House lawn hosts a free community skating rink when the temperatures drop. Each season brings new life to the outdoors.

Tip 4: Get outside.

Most of the beauty and enjoyment of Montpelier, and Vermont in general, centers around our environment. Walk, bike, or skate: however you get mobile, some of the best elements of Montpelier are seen from outside the buildings. If getting the most from your trip is your goal, then you're only seeing a fraction of the town if you don't take advantage of the many opportunities outdoors. Most of the special events and activities during the year occur outside. From sitting in on a fresh air concert or taking your coffee to a bench and people-watching to going to the Farmer's Market or lone hikes in the hills, there are options for everyone.

1.2.4 What makes Montpelier, Montpelier

When you come to Montpelier, you are entering a true, neighborly community. People here are closely connected, whether they want to be or not. We may not know our immediate neighbor very well, but our dentist/bank teller/coffee barista, etc., probably know both our kids and us. It's not six degrees of separation around here. It's more like two. This is great when you need to know someone who knows someone, but it also keeps behavior in line. You can't have a public tirade without a lot of other people you know finding out about it.

Our community tries to support our local venues, artists, and schools with the mindset that if our neighbors are thriving, they will help us to thrive as well. As a result, you will find cafés showing the artwork of local artists, schools working with local talent to provide after-school activities, churches opening their courtyards up to local musicians, businesses offering their parking lots for farmers and artisans to sell their wares, and the State House offering their lawn for many community-based events.

Being a capital city also means politics play a part in the local culture. Protests to protect individual and constitutional rights are not uncommon. You will find both sides of the aisle living as neighbors, and I like to think that that lends itself to a certain tolerance of views, despite Vermont being a left-leaning state. The simple right to being yourself is highly prized and protected as long as you don't get in the way of someone else being themself.

Tip 5: Visit award-winning Montpelier.

Montpelier is home to award-winning distilleries, bars, artists, and festivals. So if you can only spend a short time here, experience the best of the best in town by hitting up the award-winners. From local awards for restaurants and businesses (the Daisy awards, proclaimed by the Vermont newspaper Seven Days) to national awards for Barr Hill Distillery's amazing honey-tipped gin, let our finest be some of the highlights of your time here. We are even home to the studio of the award-winning art-meets-gaming toy-maker of the Pinbox 3000, featured in creative children's learning awards and magazines.

1.3 Making Your Visit Special

1.3.1 Local Events

Tip 6: Plan around local events.

Montpelier is great on its own, but there's even more small-town fun when an event brings everyone together. Don't you want to feel that small-town magic? You know you do. Frequently throughout the year, there are special events put on to bring the community together: parades, film festivals, concerts, markets, art walks, road races, and holiday celebrations, just to mention a few. If you can, add to your small-town experience by taking in at least one of these home-grown opportunities to immerse yourself like a resident of Montpelier.

Montpelier Alive, montpelieralive.com, is the main organizer/marketer of local events, so definitely compare your travel dates with their event calendar. This site also announces special sales in the local shops, has planning tools for your visit, and tons of information about the local scene.

The Bridge, montpelierbridge.org, is our small-town newspaper that gives you the inside scoop on street-level news and also the big and little events impacting the town. This is a great resource to get a feel for what's happening and what small-town life is like. They also have a cool section where they compare current buildings with what stood there when the town was first formed. Some buildings have withstood the test of time and look similar to their modern iterations, but others have changed drastically.

1.3.2 Taking Advantage of Each Season

Vermont experiences all the seasons in their full glory and adds a few more just for fun, such as stick season (where the leaves have fallen and the tree-lined hills just look like sticks) and mud season (where the dirt roads ambush your car with deep mud, sucking in your tires and your confidence that you'll make it out of there). So no matter when you are coming to Montpelier, there will be something seasonal to greet you. But seriously, please beware of the dirt roads in April.

Tip 7: Plan around the seasons.

This tip is for your comfort as well as your enjoyment. If you are not acclimated to freezing temperatures or simply don't enjoy the cold, then visiting in winter may not give you the most enjoyable experience here. Vermonters are a tough crew, but some of our winter weeks are extreme even for us.

Some events are only put on in Winter -- like our Ice On Fire Winter Festival, where our nature center crafts snow and ice sculptures, makes bonfires with donated Christmas trees and combines them much to the delight of adults and children.

If you have always wanted to see the fall foliage, then you'll want to aim for late September and early October, where "Peak Week" (the peak of the colors on the trees) is likely to hit. I always feel bad for tourist buses that arrive after Peak Week. No one can ever predict exactly when the foliage will be at its best, so they took a gamble when they booked their tickets, and sometimes they just miss the prime colors, and all that's left to photograph are the sticks.

Spring and Summer in Montpelier can fluctuate greatly in temperatures, so wear layers. The Farmers' Market on Saturday mornings comes into full swing, and fresh, seasonal fruits and vegetables start coming in, along with baked goods, pickles, pies, tinctures, salves, art, pottery, and hot, prepared foods. You can spend your whole Saturday morning and afternoon just wandering around, collecting and sampling goodies.

Whatever season you choose will have events tailored for that time of year, so you won't miss out.

1.3.3 *Live the Small-Town Life for a Day*

Those of us who enjoy living in a small town, wish everyone could have this experience. Having lived in the South for a few years and then in a New England city for a few more, coming back to Montpelier was like a sigh of relief. There is an openness and a kindness here that you don't feel in a city.

Tip 8: Enjoy the town like a local.

Living in a small town affords a unique experience, so leave your town or city behind, and immerse yourself in the friendliness of our community.

If you are coming to us from a city, take a break from the hustle and the attitude, and enjoy a more friendly connection with the people around you. Slow down. Take your coffee from Capitol Grounds and sit on a bench, and people watch as the town moseys by. Listen in to neighborly banter in the shops as you peruse unique, local finds. Ask shopkeepers or locals you can identify on the street for the best of whatever interests you. People in town like to share their advice on what's great here, and they will give you insider tips that maybe even I don't know!

Chapter Review

- Use the intersection of State Street and Main Street as your starting point. Not only is it picturesque at all times of the year, but the majority of things to do and see center around this downtown fixture.

- Stay in town. Get the most out of your stay by staying local and walking everywhere.

- Many of our best events and activities take place outside, any time of the year, so get the most out of your visit by getting outside. People often visit Vermont to see the natural environment we live in every day, so don't miss it!

- Montpelier is home to many award-winners, so if you can't stay long, make sure to hit those up first. In addition, the city event organizer, Montpelier Alive, often has up-to-date lists on their website of local winners.

- Plan around local events. Throughout the year, there are fun, educational, and family-friendly events and activities planned. Check out our local resources to see what's happening when you will be in town, or look ahead and plan your trip based on what's coming up.

- Plan around the seasons. Every season is beautiful here in its own way. What do you want to see outside? How do you want to experience Montpelier? Pick your favorite season and come see what we have to offer.

- Immersion is the best way to learn a language and experience a culture. Take a break from your usual way of life, and live ours for a time. Learn the language of the small town and experience the community where everyone knows someone you know.

Chapter 2 Welcome to Montpelier: Getting Here, Parking, and Orienting Yourself

2.1 Overview

The best way to enjoy anything is to be properly prepared for it. When it comes to travel, the foundation of your visit is going to be the practical elements: how to get there, how to settle yourself in a new place, and how to get right into the scene, so you don't miss a minute of travel adventures and enjoyment. You probably spent good money to make this happen, so let's not waste any of your investment!

2.2 Getting into Town

2.2.1 Arriving by Plane

Vermont has an international airport, although the "international" part is likely just talking about direct flights to Canada. It's a small but modern airport, and I have found it to be cleaner and nicer than some large city airports in the U.S. There are only two baggage claims when you arrive, so it's very easy to find your luggage and get on your way.

Once you have landed and have either rented a vehicle or have someone picking you up, you have two options for your drive to Montpelier: the highway, I-89, and Route 2.

Tip 9: Take Route 2 to Montpelier instead of the highway.

Route 2 runs parallel to I-89 but is much more scenic, giving you a chance to sightsee a few other small towns on your way to the Capital. Once you get further away from the airport, you will drive through farmland and see a dairy farm, a flower farm, and corn fields. Several small towns will slow your speed from 50 to 25, but just for a short while, as they are *small* towns.

A small caveat here is that since this is farmland, it is not uncommon to smell manure in the spring as the farmers prepare the land for planting. My dad always said that it smells like life to him. He's from Brooklyn, so maybe it was quite a neat novelty when he moved here. For those of us who have grown up learning to roll up our windows as we drive by a farm, the smell is not what I would call "life." But in some ways, he's not wrong: manure on farmland is the smell of self-sufficiency Vermont is known for. The cows produce it, the farmland yields better, and the farmer has a better season and more money for feeding the cows. Cue the Lion King music: *"It's the circle of liiiife...."*

Tip 10: Treat yourself to Montpelier's favorite creemee stand, Dairy Creme.

As you come into town on Route 2 in the summer, where the 50-mph speed limit reduces to 35, you will see the big DAIRY CREME sign on a small white building. It often opens around 11 am to cater to your creemee needs, especially if you've got jet-lagged kids with you. What's a creemee? You might ask since you are not from here. You might call it "soft serve" ice cream where you come from. We call it a creemee and will politely make a face if you insist on calling it otherwise.

2.2.2 Driving the Local Roads

Vermont is a French mash-up of the words *vert* (green) and *mont* (mountain), so when you are not in a town or city, you will likely be driving through a lot of the natural areas Vermont is known for. You may notice signs along the highway with the silhouette of jumping deer or the word MOOSE, which indicate that those animals frequently cross the road in that area. That is not a joke. Those signs are specifically there because state game wardens have calculated that a significant amount of hits have occurred there. Yes, we do have fences that attempt to keep wildlife out of harm's way, but these animals can jump or crush these fences, respectively. And when we're talking about moose, those hits crush cars as well.

Tip 11: When you drive at dawn, dusk, or at night, stay aware and don't speed!

I'm not warning you about cops at speed traps. I'm warning you about the wildlife. It is not uncommon to see deer crossing the road in front of you and even stopping in the road to look at the pretty approaching lights of your vehicle, so give yourself lots of time to react. You might also see skunks, raccoons, foxes, coyotes, porcupines, and on rare occasions, moose, all of which are most active at dusk and dawn and can be hard to see until they're right in front of you. The summer months are the most active for our wildlife, but you can't let your guard down until maybe winter.

Tip 12: Do not attempt to drive dirt roads in the spring unless you have 4-wheel drive and a high-clearance vehicle.

Here's the thing about dirt roads: they are beautiful to drive on, and I highly recommend finding some and enjoying the deep, wooded glades hidden on the backroads of Vermont, but there is a time and a place for it, and spring is not it. In spring, we have a mini-season called Mud Season. A dirt road in spring may look fine when you start on it, but its viability for your car making it all the way to your destination is all related to where water can pool from snow melt or rain. If the dirt road is on some high ground, it likely will look, and be, fine to drive on. But a mile down the road, where the dirt road dips into lower areas and the snow melt has accumulated along the roadside, the dirt turns into mud, and every vehicle that has traveled on it will have created deeper and deeper ruts in the mud that can destroy your car. If the ruts freeze overnight, you may try to drive on top of them to try to avoid slipping into the rut, but that's a hard skill to cultivate, and most people end up slipping off and slamming down into the rut, potentially wrecking your struts and undercarriage. On the other hand, if the ruts are warm and muddy, then you risk getting caught up in the mud and ending your travel right there, in the middle of the dirt road.

Now, the positive side to this is that Vermonters are all very aware of the risks of Mud Season, and even if you are out of cell range to call a tow truck, you will likely have the first person who finds you stop and ask if you need help. They may call a tow for you, or they may get the chains out of the back of their truck and pull you out themselves. This is not at all uncommon. I knew someone who used their Toyota Tundra and chains to pull a UPS driver out of a ditch -- people on the dirt road will help you out. But that might not be the most fun experience or story to acquire while you're here, so please, just stay off those roads in spring, a.k.a. Mud Season. Come back another time for that pastoral ride through the countryside.

2.2.3 Parking Strategies

Once you have landed in Montpelier, you will need to park your vehicle. If you are staying at one of the hotels or inns in town, you will have access to free parking on-site. But if you are coming in for the day, here are a few considerations about where to park.

Montpelier has started using the ParkMobile app to pay for parking in different zones in the downtown area. I have found the app easy to set up and use; the signage downtown is pretty visible, and easy to identify what zone you are in. However, you pay a price for this convenience, which is why I recommend the following:

Tip 13: Have change for metered parking.

It is cheaper than using the ParkMobile App to pay for parking in town. For $.25, you can park for 15 minutes. So, $1.00 for an hour of parking. On the ParkMobile app, that fee will be more like $1.60 for an hour. But if you're staying most of the day, maybe you want an even better deal.

Tip 14: Free parking is found just a bit outside the downtown area.

If you are used to walking a block or two to get around or don't mind a 5–10 minute stroll, then you may want to consider parking in an adjacent neighborhood to avoid paying for parking. It won't take long to walk from any neighborhood to get downtown. I will probably hear from my neighbors that I am suggesting taking parking spots residents may use, but it is an option, and on super busy event days/nights, you may have no choice but to park in those neighborhood areas just to find a spot. School Street and Park Avenue are my immediate go-to streets to find free parking, and it's still close to the shops and restaurants.

Tip 15: Pay attention to the winter parking ban signs.

These signs are posted in many of those same neighborhoods where you would like to park for free. You will see signs that direct you on which side of the street to park and at which times so that the plows can clear the other side of the road. When everyone adheres to these times, the roads are well-plowed for everyone's safety.

Tip 16: Free parking after 5 pm on weekdays and during the entire weekend.

After 5 pm, you don't have to worry about paying parking meters or having parking stickers to park in the State Employee parking lots, most of which are located behind the State Street buildings. State employees get off work at 4:30 pm, so these can be easy places to park downtown after they leave.

2.3 Safety

This is a pretty safe city, so if you forget to lock your car doors while you're out and about during the day, nothing will likely happen to your car. At night, though, it's smart to take your usual precautions just because, but generally, it's a very safe town at all times. Our local newspaper, The Times Argus www.timesargus.com, often publishes the local Police Logs if you'd like to see what gets called in on a regular basis. It's usually a mix of traffic stops, a dog loose or barking, a lost wallet turned in, "suspicious activity," and someone painting graffiti.

2.4 Areas and Features of the Town

2.4.1 Natural Features

Montpelier is defined by its location in a valley, in the midst of several hills, with a few rivers or tributaries weaving through. Vermonters will often use natural features or unique structures to give directions, so it's good to know what these are if you ask for help. One easy way to orient yourself in town is to get a map!

Tip 17: Find the Visitor's Center or the Information Kiosk, both located on State Street, and pick up a Discovery Map.

This cute, hand-drawn map will give you up-to-date locations of our restaurants, shops, and public spaces.

The Visitor's Center is located at 134 State St, Montpelier, VT 05602

The Information Kiosk is located next to the Christ Episcopalian Church across from Elm Street.

There are two main rivers that cross through Montpelier. The North Branch River, which runs under the downtown area, connects to the Winooski River, which runs parallel to the aptly named River Street, which is the road you will be on when you get off the highway. River Street is just outside what I would consider downtown, where most of our gas stations are located.

Tip 18: Winooski is Abenaki (the Native American tribe from this region) for Wild Onion, so you may notice some references to Onion, or the Onion River, in town.

In the spring, as the river ice starts to break up, Montpelier watches the line of ice intently as it starts to compact and rise. Twice, Montpelier has flooded due to a spring season with intense rain, while warm temperatures helped the thawing snow melt quickly and drain into the river. As the ice broke up and compacted into bridges and low outcroppings of trees, the water could not flow freely downstream and rose over the banks and into downtown Montpelier.

The first flood was in 1927, and it sent water more than 14 feet over the flood stage and killed almost 100 people.

The second flood was in 1992, while I was in 8th grade. In this flood, there was no loss of life, and the high water mark reached 3-4 feet above street level. Everyone had gone to school and work that day without issue, and perhaps some people had looked at the ice shoring up against the river banks and thought with amazement, "Wow, look at that!" But within a few more hours, the banks would flow over into the streets, concentrating in downtown Montpelier and shuttering all businesses, swamping unfortunate vehicles, and forcing the schools to call parents and release kids to find their way home.

My mom had picked up my younger brother and sister from the elementary school, and my friend and I went to meet them and go home. I remember attempting to cross the street to meet my mom and being met with deeper and deeper water, not realizing how much flooding was really happening and how much water I was stepping into. My mom carried my brother and sister over to my side instead, and we found my mom's car somehow not parked in the waterlogged downtown next to her office.

Two people from our high school had their pictures taken canoeing down Main Street, and while we are all told now not to consider going for a joyride during a flood, I can't help but feel like that was a once-in-a-lifetime opportunity that I would probably take.

2.4.2 Neighborhoods

Walking around the neighborhoods of downtown Montpelier is one of my favorite things to do. It's an easy walk, it gets you away from most traffic, and the homes are all so interesting to look at as you walk by. Especially if you are not from New England, these neighborhoods each bring to life their own quintessential perspective of small, New England town charm.

The Meadows

Just off Elm Street, walking away from the State House and the downtown area, the Meadows neighborhood begins with Spring Street and encompasses Summer Street, Winter Street, Vine Street, and Pearl Street.

I know what you're thinking. Where is Fall Street? Or Autumn Avenue? That seasonal street is simply not one of the options.

Why is it called the Meadows? Well, like most of Montpelier in the beginning, it was a field when the first homes were built. Specifically, this meadow was settled by the Hubbard family, after which the adjacent land of Hubbard Park was named. For many years as the town grew, it was called Hubbard's Meadow. As the land slowly built up into a full neighborhood, with the remnants of the meadow being the small yards adjacent to the houses, the name Hubbard was sufficiently transferred to the park, and the neighborhood shortened its moniker to "the meadows."

This is the neighborhood you think of when you imagine kids playing in the streets and riding bikes in safety, where the neighbors know each other or know their neighbor's kids because of all the playing and biking. And yard sales abound in the summertime! Someone is having a yard sale at any given moment in the summer.

There is also an access point to Hubbard Park in this neighborhood. Just look for where the streets start to have an incline, and you'll naturally end up in the park. There are actually two entrance points that take you to the same entrance at the end. One is right off Spring Street, called Parkway Street, and takes a gentler slope most of the way up. The other is off of Winter Street, and that is a more severe incline but a shorter way to the main entrance.

Liberty Street/Loomis Street/Marvin Street

Across from the Meadows neighborhood, next to Birchgrove Bakery, there is a footbridge over a little running waterfall of the North Branch River.

Tip 19: Meet the Lane Shops: Montpelier's former major manufacturing center of the world's sawmill equipment in the late 1800s.

The red apartments running alongside the footbridge are the modern form for these old buildings where Dennis Lane produced and internationally distributed lever-set circular saws that made cutting lumber faster and more accurate.

Once you have crossed the footbridge, head right down Franklin Street, and cross the road to Liberty Street. This street, along with its crossroad, Loomis Street, showcases another conglomeration of homes much like the Meadows. Here, the street can be a little busier as many locals use it as a way to get to the other side of town without going through the downtown traffic light. More examples of Victorian architecture are interspersed here, and more sprawling farmhouses, examples of how family homes were built extending sections onto the original frame and created very long buildings in small lots.

Tip 20: Take in the different paint schemes.

Victorian architecture isn't the only example of contrasting color schemes to bring attention to detail. These streets have many examples of simpler designs using color, stone, and glass to enhance their curb appeal, making this neighborhood walk very eye-catching.

Vermont College Neighborhoods

A combination of College Street, Hinkley Street, McKinley Street, Arsenal Drive, First Avenue, and Kent Street starts at the top of Liberty Street, where you run into College Street, named after Vermont College, which will be down the road to your right. You can walk towards the college directly or take a loop around Hinkley/McKinley/Arsenal Drive, which is right across from the top of Liberty Street.

College Street is filled with Victorian homes and some more modern, colonial-style houses. As you get closer to Vermont College, right at the end of Arsenal Drive, you will see a very small, out-of-place brick home with an enclosed porch that sits further away from the road. This is the last arsenal standing from the original three buildings Montpelier stocked during the Civil War.

Cut across the green of Vermont College, and you will find two related, historic streets to peruse. First Avenue, a steep drop/hike, depending on the direction you take it, continues the Victorian theme with more examples of these statuesque homes. Kent Street, a little side street further down and behind the college from First Avenue, is an eclectic mix of architectural styles and sizes and really has to be seen to understand. Besides a little home that looks like a mini-Victorian, there is the former Kent family home with its unique, circular porch frame. The Kent family was one of the original big names in Montpelier, with one of the sons later becoming the city historian, chronicling many of the events of mid-19th century Montpelier.

Terrace Street Area

Across town, on the other side of the Capitol building, is Bailey Avenue, which leads to Terrace Street and, further up, Clarendon Avenue. When the city was first populating, homes naturally were built closer to the city center, so on these streets, the largest and most visually impressive homes were the first 4-5 houses. Those are the Victorian houses again and a few brick mansions. As the incline gets steeper and further away from downtown, the homes become more conventional and modern, so if you're walking, be aware that the intrigue will settle down after that.

Chapter Review

- Take Route 2 from Burlington International Airport to Montpelier. It is more scenic, lands you right on State Street, and you can get a creemee right on your way in.

- It's a creemee here, not soft-serve ice cream. Of course, you can call it soft-serve if you want, but just know we are all quietly identifying you as the tourist you are.

- Find a Discovery Map at the Montpelier Visitor Center at 134 State Street or the Information booth at State Street and Elm.

- If you don't have change for the meters, use the ParkMobile App, or park a little further away for free in the neighborhoods.

- Slow down and stay aware when you drive at night. Wildlife is active.

- Don't drive on the dirt roads in the spring.

- The neighborhoods directly adjacent to the downtown have a ton of well-kept architectural examples of the early buildings in town.

Chapter 3 Montpelier is For Kids

3.1 Overview

A lot of people who grow up here return to start families and raise their kids in this family-friendly, outdoorsy, healthy town. I am certainly one of them. It may be a small town, but opportunities to entertain and, dare I say, also educate the younger members of the community are abundant.

3.2 Treats for the Kids

If you're a travel-savvy parent, then you know that one of the make-or-break elements of your trip has to be when and where the kids eat. I find it to be a particularly good motivator for getting to the next part of the day when the kids know something special is waiting for them when they get there. So let's load you up with an arsenal of options to keep the kids happy!

3.2.1 Ice Cream, Gelato, Creemees, Smoothies, and Milkshakes

Where the Skinny Pancake now resides used to be a Ben & Jerry's Scoop Shop. It was a sad day when the quintessential ice cream of Vermont moved out of the Capital City. It was one of the few, if not the only, place to get hard ice cream. If you're in Vermont and want the full Ben & Jerry's experience, I'm going to assume that you'll be visiting the factory in Waterbury, just 20 minutes north of Montpelier. In fact, you passed it on your way from the airport.

Otherwise, in Montpelier, you will have other less famous, but just as delicious, frozen treat options.

First is the Dairy Creme, which you passed when you took Route 2 from the airport. If you were in a rush that day, though, and took the highway, the Dairy Creme is an easy find. Just find the State House on State Street, and then take that street, headed away from the downtown shops.

You'll pass the Green Mountain Cemetery (with a few haunted spots I'll tell you about later), and then Dairy Creme will be on your left. Unfortunately, this place is only open in the warmer months -- usually, opening day is at the end of May, and closing is at the beginning of September.

Tip 21: Try the Dish of Dirt.

Vanilla (or chocolate) ice cream with hot fudge, crushed Oreo layers, and a gummy worm on top to complete the look of a dish of dirt; it is very popular.

If you're on the other side of town, maybe coming back from a Mountaineers game or the North Branch Nature Center, you can get your creemee fix at Meadow Mart. This little neighborhood convenience store has been open for over 40 years.

Tip 22: The best Maple Creemee you can get year-round is at Morse's Farm, just on the border of Montpelier and East Montpelier.

Sure, lots of creemee stands in Vermont will offer a maple-flavored creemee, but trust me on this, it is not the same as a maple creemee from Morse's. I will say that maybe other maple sugar producers have a decent maple creemee that can still outshine a gas station creemee, but I know for a fact that Morse's is using some full-cream deliciousness for their creemee starter. Add to that their real maple syrup produced on site that year, and you'll understand why I am pointing them out in particular.

To get there, start driving on State Street, away from the downtown and away from the river (you don't cross any rivers to get to Morse's), and just keep going. You'll eventually see signs for Morse's, but essentially, you just keep driving until you see it on your right.

Tip 23: Try Sugar On Snow!

In the early spring, you can also take the kids to Morse's Farm for the unique experience of Sugar On Snow, which is boiling hot maple syrup poured over hard-packed fresh snow. The reaction between the boiled maple syrup and the icy snow creates a maple-flavored, taffy-like candy. To balance all that sugar out, the classic accoutrements to Sugar On Snow are a dill pickle and fluffy cider donut, which you can order with your sugar.

Tip 24: Order maple to go.

Want to bring all that maple goodness from Morse's Farm home but don't want to carry gallons of syrup or boxes and boxes of candy? Morse's Farm has online ordering and can take your order at the store and ship it to your home, so Montpelier's finest is waiting for you upon your return. Maple candy makes a great gift, and Vermont maple syrup will blow your store-bought "maple flavored" syrup out of the water. A quick note: Grade A syrup will be lighter in color and flavor, maybe even a little sweeter than Grade B, which will be darker and more robust. Morse's Farm often puts out tasting syrups, so you can try them first.

Closer to the center of town, you can find a small-batch, in-house gelato shop called Chill on State Street. Friendly service and authentic and unique flavors attract kids and adults alike throughout the year, but especially in the summer, where Chill is a perfect place for an after-lunch or dinner dessert.

Across the street from Chill is Capitol Grounds, which offers dairy-free (and dairy-full) fruit smoothies. I love the strawberry smoothie with yogurt, but mango is my daughters' choice.

Tip 25: Try the Mocha Chill from Capitol Grounds if you want a super chocolate-coffee milkshake.

But the best milkshakes in town are at the burger joint Buddy's Famous Burgers. Classic flavors are exactly as you remember them, but it's the special flavors that everyone wants: Fruity Pebbles, Shamrock Mint, Nutella, and Reese's are just some of the fun concoctions they make.

3.2.2 Candy

Imagine my surprise when I went to hunt down candy stores in all of Vermont and came up with just a handful in the state. Shockingly disappointing. Thankfully, Montpelier is one of those cities that offers a candy store, and despite its tiny size, Delish has a solid range of classic penny candies, gummies, bulk bins, JellyBelly flavors, truffles, maple candy, and Vermont-based chocolates.

3.2.3 Boba Tea

Boba is not my cup of tea (har, har), but apparently, it is very popular with the youth. While I do not enjoy drinking and then chewing something from a drink, my daughters do not seem to mind the chewy or popping varieties in their fruity beverages. So if your kids get excited for Boba, let me direct you to Capital Pho on State Street. This is the go-to place local kids like to get their Boba fix.

3.3 Our Best Family-Friendly Activities

3.3.1 Playgrounds

Need to run off some energy? Playgrounds are so great for that because the kids can just run around in a fairly enclosed, safe location, and you can finally sit down, if you're lucky. Who has kids who don't yell for a push on the swing or for us to meet them at the top of the climbing structure? None of us, that's who. So sit for that short moment, while you can.

My childhood haunt is the playground at Union Elementary School on Park Avenue. This playground is very close to downtown and has two levels that offer age-appropriate equipment for small to big kids. There are also small fields to run around on, swings and slides, and an award-winning architectural play structure called The Birds Nest. My favorite is the huge climbing structure made of massive ropes. And yes, it's my favorite because I've climbed all over it. Gotta test these things out, right?

Another close playground is located behind the T.W. Wood Art Gallery on Barre Street. This playground has hosted children from multiple different school iterations on site, which originally was St. Michael's Catholic school, conveniently located next to St. Augustine's Catholic Church. This playground has great slides -- one of which is tall and twisty and two that are great for speed.

Tip 26: This playground on Barre Street is very close to Buddy's Famous Burgers, so it's a great option for a light lunch and some playtime for the kids to get them happy and tired out during your stay.

If you end up going to the Mountaineers games, or the Rec Pool on Elm Street, there is a playground by the pool. It's a bit of a walk from the middle of town, so usually, there are not many kids here except when the pool is open, so this is a good option if you are planning to hike some trails around that area or need to give your kids a break from the crowds.

3.3.2 The Farmers Market

While the Farmers Market runs year-round now, the best time to bring the kids is during the summer market season, which starts in May and runs through October, 9 am-1 pm. In the summer, the Farmers Market has been setting up in a parking lot near the State House. You'll have no problem finding it.

During the summer, there can be live music, a Kids' Market where local children sell their wares (and it's awesome), an ice cream cart complete with a little bell, picnic tables to take your fresh foods, and so many dogs (on leashes, of course)!

My strategy to you: Do a first lap around the market to note the vendors you like, then go back and dive into purchasing those local goods. Although I will admit, kids generally don't have my patience. When I go to the market with my daughters, they don't want to walk past their favorite foods, they want to eat that deliciousness now, and I can't blame them.

So here is my revised strategy: Get your kids set up with the foods they like and settle them on a grassy spot to eat. If they are old enough to be left comfortably alone for a little while, let them eat while you go back and shop. If they aren't that independent yet, sate them with the food they like, and then go back out with them to shop with the promise of a few dollars for ice cream or a treat to bring home. Give them a mission that will be completed once you have what you want. You're paying for all this, after all! You get what you want!

Tip 27: Hit up the prepared food vendors at the end of the market and maybe score a deal!

Many of these vendors would rather sell the last of their prepared foods at a discount, or give you a whole lot of it at the usual price, than pack it all up and bring it home. You risk your favorites being gone, but if you don't mind taking a chance or buying something new or different, you can get a really good deal.

There used to be a potsticker vendor that I *loved* so much I would go every Saturday with a reusable container and buy a ton of her potstickers. OMG, they were so good. One day I got there as they were closing up. I rushed to her stall and asked if she had any potstickers left. She had a few, but because it was the end of the market, and maybe because she knew I was a repeat customer, she loaded me up with noodles and egg rolls as well, all for the price of a few potstickers. Worth it!

3.3.3 Mountaineers Games

Tip 28: Go to a Mountaineers game!

During the summer, you may see signs for Mountaineers games. This is a great activity for the family. The Mountaineers are our local baseball team, made up of college-aged baseball stars in the making. Local families host these kids for the summer, and everyone enjoys going to the games. Kids will enjoy the game, the local treats offered at food trucks and stadium vendors, and running around with other kids on the adjacent fields. The organizers often also have kids come out onto the field for mini-games between innings. One favorite is the Toss-A-Ball challenge, where kids get baseballs and try to throw them into the Mountaineers team car that drives slowly down the third baseline. One of the few times you can throw a ball at a car and not get in trouble! Kids get a prize if they make it in!

Tip 29: Go to the game early to park close to the field.

Parking for the Mountaineers games can be costly and crowded, especially closer to the field. Go early if you want a prime spot.

If having your car nearby is not a dealbreaker for you, it's just as easy, if not easier, to catch the local bus that stops around town to pick people up and drop them off right at the park. These temporary bus stops - or Skip Stops, named after the team mascot - are well-marked in town.

Walking or biking is also an option for attending a game, but it's at least 20 minutes walking from downtown. If you have young kids, this might be asking too much. Bikes, scooters, or electric skateboards would be much easier.

3.3.4 Skatepark

Speaking of the ballpark, another physical and outdoor activity you or your kids might enjoy is the local skatepark, which is located behind the ballpark. It's not a big skatepark by any means, but it has some rails and ramps to ride on. I have taken my girls there on scooters, skateboards, and electric skateboards. It's usually pretty quiet there. Anyone already riding when you get there will generally just leave you alone - this is not usually a busy park as it is a little further outside of town for kids to get to.

3.3.5 The Public Pool -aka- The Rec Pool

While you're at the Rec Fields for the Mountaineers game or to check out the skate park, you will also notice the public pool, which is fondly called The Rec Pool (short for Recreation Center Pool).

Tip 30: This pool is the largest concrete, sloping-side pool still in use in the U.S.!

The gentle slope into the water makes this pool great for families with kids of all ages. There is also a long metal railing that glides down into the water from the edge to assist those with disabilities. Fully staffed with trained lifeguards who enforce the rules with loud whistles and speakers, this pool offers a place to cool off, play, lounge in the sun, and get some snacks. Super littles can play in the bubblers in the shallowest depths by the edge while mom and dad sit in the water with them. Older kids who are proficient swimmers can get right into the deep middle of the pool, where there are concrete platforms to jump from. The platform of diving boards is called The Tower. It may not look like much, but when you're up there, it's a long way down!

3.3.6 North Branch Nature Center

A wonderful, natural gem still in Montpelier, but further down the road from the ballpark, is the North Branch Nature Center. Recent upgrades have made this space a beautiful, rustic, but modern haven for nature lovers. They run programs year-round that take advantage of the natural ebbs and flows of the seasons and also of the North Branch rivulet that runs along and through the land.

Tip 31: Try all of the walking paths.

One of the paths leads up into a little forested area that has been built up by kids in the Forest Preschool program, complete with a little rope swing. Several paths will lead to little entry points to play in the river. The path with the bridge will take you away from the Nature Center and ends up back at the Rec Fields, where the skatepark, ballpark, and public pool are located.

3.3.7 *Kellogg-Hubbard Library*

If it's a gray day and you have young kids with you, Kellogg-Hubbard Library has a children's library upstairs with toys, train sets, doll houses, and, of course, books.

Tip 32: The children's library has a clean bathroom and a changing table.

It also allows for speaking voices, so you don't have to silence your kids. You're welcome.

The library will often have reading circles, crafts, and other kids' programming during the week.

3.3.8 *Valentine's Day*

While not really an activity for kids, Valentine's Day in Montpelier is notorious for its magic and wonder. Years ago, one morning, we all woke up to find the town plastered in red hearts. 8x11 papers printed with big, shiny red hearts had been adhered to doors, windows, lamp posts, walls, and whatever other surfaces the Valentine Phantom could reach all over State Street and Main Street. The hearts continued to mysteriously appear every year after, slowly growing in size and locations. Banners encircled the State House columns, and large hearts were hung over bridges. Even the tower of Vermont College was graced with an enormous paper heart.

However, one Valentine's Day, there were no hearts downtown, and immediately, everyone was concerned for the health of the Phantom, and I think that moment also made the town recognize how much they loved this tradition. So, answering the call of an unexpectedly distraught town, a group of high school students took it upon themselves to uphold the tradition, printed their own hearts, and hung them around town in the afternoon.

Ever since that year, the Valentine's Day Phantom has become a community event, with children at school coloring large hearts that a group of secret individuals will then add to their own prints and hang all over town before dawn. It has become a special honor for local kids to go find where their heart was placed in town. No one wants to wake up again to a town without those symbols of love.

3.3.9 The Annual Easter Egg Hunt

The Saturday before Easter Sunday, there is a free community Easter Egg hunt in Hubbard Park hosted by the Montpelier Recreation Center. The gates to the park will open at 9:45 am, allowing the throngs of children and their parents to hike up the main road to find the area associated with their age range. The youngest are the closest to the entrance, with the older kids trudging farther up. The "hunting areas" are cordoned off with ropes and brightly colored tape, creating a rough circle of hunting grounds. Then, at 10 am sharp, a loud horn will blow, indicating that it is time to cross the roped barrier and race your peers to all the colorful chocolate eggs on the ground.

Tip 33: Encourage your child(ren) to walk around towards the side of their designated area, furthest away from the road.

Most kids and parents line up right next to the road at first because it's so convenient. However, it then becomes a question of supply and demand, and when 20 kids are lined up all on one side, the supply is going to dwindle fast when the horn blows. So give your kid the best chance at a solid chocolate haul by moving up the sides of the area toward the back, where fewer kids go.

Tip 34: Look for the Gold and Silver eggs!

In every age group, there is a large gold egg and a large silver egg hidden amongst the forest flora. It could be up a tree, under a tree, or covered with some leaves... but if you find it, you are entitled to a special Easter gift basket back at the entrance to the park! Always be on the lookout for those, but don't miss the chocolate that's easier to find on the ground.

3.3.10 Independence Day Celebration

While Independence Day is officially July 4th, Montpelier holds its celebrations on July 3rd. Most of State Street is blocked off, creating a wide thoroughfare for revelers. The day features lots of games, dances, and live music on the State House lawn, and food trucks selling wide ranges of foods from pizza and sausages to BBQ and Mediterranean. Vendors also sell balloons, face-painting sessions, ice cream, and glow-in-the-dark toys and necklaces. Before the parade down Main and State Street at 6 pm, there is a 1-mile fun run down these two major thoroughfares through town, with everyone in town cheering you on from the sidelines! Fireworks usually start around 9:30 pm.

Tip 35: For the best seats in the house, set up your blanket or chairs on the right side of the State House lawn, as you're facing *away* from the State House building.

Kids with sensitive ears may want to have ear protection or watch further away from the Capitol building because the booming sound of the fireworks echoes off the building walls.

3.3.11 Montpelier Fall Festival

Montpelier Fall Festival is held in October and features lots of games on the State House lawn. It also brings in face painters, food trucks, and live music to keep everyone in your family entertained.

The proceeds from this event go directly to support the schools in the district, giving all kids a helpful boost by ensuring field trips, guest speakers, and special school-community events to enhance the children's education and growth.

3.3.12 Halloween

You don't have to dress up to thoroughly enjoy Halloween in Montpelier! Hey, you don't even have to be here on Halloween to enjoy it!

Tip 36: If you visit Montpelier in the weeks approaching Halloween, check out "The Halloween House" on College Street in the evening.

This house on the far end of College Street (furthest away from Vermont College) boasts a huge collection of spooky decor arranged over the lawn and even up the sides of the house.

Fun fact: It was actually the house next to it that started the tradition. Bob (one of Montpelier's fantastic resident on-call plumbers) and his wife started collecting and putting up new decorations every year for over 30 years before they passed on the tradition to their willing neighbors.

On Halloween night, to address the influx of visitors to the house, the police block the top of the road and set officers to direct traffic at the very busy intersection. That section of the street becomes a little Halloween block party with trick-or-treaters and sightseers wandering all over in a dark night, fluorescent LED-lit daze.

Tip 37: If you are visiting on Halloween night, bring your kids to the Downtown Trick-or-Treating from 4-5:30 pm.

Local businesses will hand out candy outside their doors, and because it's not dark out yet, you can see everyone's costumes really well. Some people get very creative. Even if you don't have kids yourself, this is a very entertaining parade of costumes to watch.

If you want to people-watch this spectacle instead of navigating the swarms of superheroes and spooks, I would recommend the window seats of Charlie O's or Positive Pie. This will give you prime viewing real estate, along with a drink and maybe some food. Three Penny Taproom windows are also an option, but they are a little further away from the fun, so they will be decent but not as "in the thick of it" as the first options.

3.3.13 *All Species Day*

If your kid loves animals, look up All Species Day in Montpelier. This is a sweet, small parade and gathering of kids and adults who love animals and come together dressed as their favorites. It's part of our small-town charm; you can see how happy the kids are to wear wings, antennae, and paws. Note: This is NOT a Furry convention.

3.3.14 *New Year's Eve*

To celebrate the end of the year, Montpelier holds its own New Year's Eve celebrations.

Tip 38: During the day and into the early evening, there are lots of activities for kids - such as live music, entertainers, arts-and-crafts, and usually fireworks around 8 pm.

Tip 39: If it's super cold out, park your car in the lots behind the State Employee office buildings, facing away from the buildings.

It will seem as though you are just looking at a snowy, wooded hillside, but when the fireworks start, you will have a warm viewing spot for the fireworks. National Life Insurance Company, perched at the top of that hillside, allows the use of their parking garage for setting up and setting off the city's fireworks, so you will be in the right place for cold weather entertainment.

Chapter Review

- The best maple creemee is at Morse's Farm.

- Try Sugar-on-Snow at Morse's Farm in the early spring for a once-a-year treat during sugaring season.

- Mountaineers games are family-friendly events that the kids love.

- If you don't want to go super early to the game to get nearby parking (that you still have to pay for), wait for a shuttle at one of the Skip Stops in town for a free ride to and from the game.

- In summer, spend some time at the largest in-ground, sloping concrete pools in the United States: the Montpelier Rec Pool on Elm Street, in the same area as the Mountaineers Ballpark.

- The big, city-wide celebrations are July 3rd and early October for the Fall Festival, Halloween, and New Year's Eve.

Chapter 4 Montpelier is For Adults

4.1 Overview

We can't let the kids have all the fun, can we? Montpelier has lots of options for a parents' night out, a group of friends out on the town, or a single traveler looking to immerse themselves in the nightlife.

4.2 Mountaineers (again!)

The Mountaineers games aren't just for the kids. Actually, I would say the demographics at the games are split almost 50/50. So check out a game to break up your day from all the site-seeing and shopping you've been doing.

Tip 40: There is a beer garden along the first baseline! Need I say more?

There are also food trucks and vendors below the stands that sell the classic ballpark foods you expect, as well as some surprises. So if you're into baseball or just want something fun to do surrounded by cheering, lively, friendly fans, this is a great activity to join.

Tip 41: Games usually start around 5:30 and go until 8:30/9:00 pm. Some even end with fireworks!

Hopefully, you also saw my note on parking for the games in the last chapter, but if not, a quick reminder: Parking near the venue fills up fast, so go early if you want your car close by. Otherwise, find a "Skip Stop" downtown and pick up a free shuttle bus that will take you to and from the park.

4.3 Live Music

4.3.1 Christ Church Courtyard

Tip 42: Go to the Episcopalian church on State Street during summer weekdays for a free lunchtime concert.

It's called the Brown Bag Series, often sponsored by different local businesses, and welcomes people during their lunch hour to sit in the church courtyard and enjoy folk music, rock, blues, and jazz.

4.3.2 Hugo's Piano Bar

You can find the Piano Bar at Hugo's open for live entertainment on Thursday, Friday, and Saturday nights.

Tip 43: Get dinner in the restaurant below first -- Hugo's makes great dumplings and summer rolls - but really, everything is good on their menu.

4.3.2 The Bent Nail

The Bent Nail on Langdon Street also offers live music, a small dance space, and solid drinks at the bar.

4.3.4 Charlie O's

Charlie-O's offers live music throughout the week, with a Karaoke Night on Tuesdays and Open Mic/Jams on Sundays. The music ranges widely from beachy ska to metal to DJ'ed dance party, so look them up to see what's playing.

Tip 44: Charlie-O's is a cash-only bar.

4.4 Getting a Drink

4.4.1 Three Penny Taproom

Love beer? Then Three Penny Taproom is where you want to go. Boasting a long list of rotating and permanent craft brews, it also serves excellent pub food to complement your drink. They also craft a good cocktail if beer isn't your thing.

Tip 45: The best seats are in the windows so you can people-watch while you imbibe.

This is a very popular spot for the after-work crowd, especially when the State Legislature is in session at the State House, so plan accordingly if you want a quieter experience or want to get a seat without waiting.

4.4.2 Charlie O's

Are you more of a dive bar fan? You can't get any more dive than our long-lived Charlie-O's.

Tip 46: Its biker-bar history is pasted on its walls in the form of old pictures, record covers, and posters dating back to the 1970s.

While Charlie-O's used to be lined with leather-clad bikers, it is now known as a "dive for nice people." Be aware of the low ceilings, tiny bathrooms, and cash-only bar. There are two pool tables to enjoy as well. Again, the best seats in the house while you drink your PBR are the window seats, which have been newly replaced with larger panes that can open in the summer. A dive bar with fresh air? Of course, you find that in Vermont...

4.4.3 Barr Hill Distillery

Besides winning Double Gold at the New York International Spirits
Competition, and Best Gin of the Year at the Hong Kong
International Spirits Competition, Caledonia Spirits' Barr Hill Gin
is the first spirit ever to receive a perfect score of 100 at the 2020
USA Spirits Ratings. Out of 586 entrants that year, representing 45
countries, our very own Caledonia Spirits' Barr Hill Gin not only
won first place but also earned a score that no spirit had achieved
before.

So if craft cocktails are more your thing, then head away from the
downtown area on Barre Street to find Caledonia Spirits' Barr Hill
Distillery. They offer unique drinks using their award-winning
liquors and delicious food to pair with them. During the summer,
take your drink and food outside to their open lawn, or enjoy inside
in their open, well-lit bar area after a self-tour of their distillery.

 It was one of the first cocktails created using their award-winning
honey-hinted gin, and it is delicious! You will be ready to invest in a
bottle or two after you have one!

Barr Hill Distillery is off of the bike path that runs through
Montpelier. It is a bit more of a walk to get to than the rest of
downtown Montpelier.

4.5 Cannabis

Recreational cannabis is now legal, and we have a dispensary right
in town at Capital Cannabis, as well as a dispensary a little outside
of downtown, on River Street, called Gram Central Station.
Vermont dispensaries will offer strains of flowers grown locally and
often in small batches. So yes, even our weed is artisan and hand-
crafted. Here are the legalities you need to know:

Tip 47: Have your I.D. ready, and pay attention to the signage.

Legal, recreational dispensaries are fairly new to Vermont, with the first licenses to open businesses being granted in September 2022. Since policies and procedures are still new and being adjusted to meet the reality of running this new type of business, it's a good idea to read any signs out front so you are aware of changes that could affect your visit. For example, they may be cash-only while they line up taking debit cards. Also, there may be a limit to how many people are allowed in at once.

Etiquette in these businesses, basically, I can sum this up with:

Tip 48: Act as if this isn't a big deal.

Do you go into a liquor store and make stupid jokes about how drunk you could get in there? I hope not. You're an adult, aren't you? Do you go into a convenience store and ask the clerk if they ever smoke the cigarettes they sell? Who would do that? So don't do it in the dispensaries. Be cool.

Tip 49: Don't smoke cannabis in public. It is illegal.

Now, I'm going to be honest with you, that does not stop people from smoking in public sometimes, and occasionally you will walk past someone and get a real whiff of whatever they just smoked. I find blatant public smoking to be kind of an obnoxious and unnecessary flaunting of the rules - we just got this new privilege; please don't ruin it for everyone because you feel entitled to smoke wherever it pleases you. So let me offer some realistic advice: Just don't smoke your newly purchased flower where people are. Smoke in your car parked away from public eyes and away from state buildings (which often have security officers walking the grounds), take a walk in the woods or eat some THC gummies instead. Until we are licensed for cannabis cafés, these are your other not-blatant options for getting high in the capital city. Oh, and to those who vape and think they're so sneaky:

Tip 50: Your vape still smells like weed.

Maybe some people can't smell it, but I can. And I don't judge you for smoking, but I do judge you for thinking you're the exceptional vaping talent who can fool the world. And if you're thinking, "I'm not trying to fool anyone, I just don't care, and I do what I want," I'm now judging you for never having grown out of that juvenile phase of self-centered thoughtlessness.

Chapter Review

- Mountaineers games have a beer garden along the first baseline.

- Hugo's Restaurant has a piano bar upstairs that opens Thursday, Friday, and Saturday evenings.

- The Bent Nail has live music and a small dance floor.

- Charlie O's offers live music, Karaoke night, and a cash-only bar.

- Three Penny Taproom has the widest craft beer selection.

- Barr Hill Distillery uses its award-winning craft liquors to create fabulous cocktails and has great food to pair with them.

- Recreational cannabis is now legal to buy in the dispensaries in town but illegal to smoke in public.

Chapter 5 Where to Eat, What to Eat

5.1 Overview

I don't know about you, but I plan my travel around food. I scout out restaurants in advance to analyze their menus, their formality - or lack thereof - and their prices. So, to save you time and energy when you visit Montpelier, I went ahead and did some of the leg work for you.

5.2 Best Breakfasts

5.2.1 Kismet

Located on Barre Street, Kismet is open for brunch Sunday's 10-2 pm. It is a very small establishment, so it is smart to make a reservation ahead of time so you don't risk waiting outside for a table only to find that they can't take you.

Tip 51: Get the Bread Pudding or the Portuguese Baked Eggs.

They both are comfort food meets deep, rich flavor. But honestly, Kismet puts so much attention to quality that I doubt you'll go wrong with anything on their menu. Add a Mimosa, and brunch is served!

5.2.2 Oakes & Evelyn

For another option for brunch, check out Oakes & Evelyn on State Street every Sunday from 10-2 pm. This restaurant is quickly becoming known for its upscale menu offerings and dedication to quality. Just taking a look at their menu, I want to eat everything.

5.2.3 Capitol Grounds

For a quick breakfast pick-up any day of the week, go to Capitol Grounds for their small-batch roasted coffees, fair trade teas, and freshly baked goods. They also have a solid breakfast sandwich menu and lunch fare as well. My recommendation for breakfast is the Green Eggs & Ham, which features pesto on local bread with a fried egg and ham.

Tip 52: Capitol Grounds also has the best BLT in town, both in price and taste. Their version is called the ABC (Avocado, Bacon, Cheddar). The best.

Capitol Grounds is quite popular and, therefore, busy when people are heading to work around 8 am and at lunchtime. Take advantage of the window seats, or bring your coffee outside and score one of the bistro tables set up by the sidewalk.

5.2.4 Bohemian Bakery

For a quieter café to enjoy coffee, tea, quiche, and delightful pastries, Bohemian Bakery delivers on all fronts. Its newly renovated space is clean, light, and open. You're probably tired of me talking about window seats, but I have to make a special mention here. These are the best window seats in the whole town! Looking down State Street, you can see the entire intersection and people-watch the pedestrians walking from all directions. In my opinion, this is the best entertainment while you sip coffee and tuck into a custard danish.

5.2.5 Birchgrove Bakery

Located on Elm Street, on your way to the Rec Fields, is Birchgrove Bakery. This location was originally a bakery called Gesine's and was famously owned by Sandra Bullock's sister. Now with new owners and a new name, this shop puts out a dazzling display of fancy desserts and simple favorites, as well as freshly brewed coffee and tea.

Tip 53: Go early on Sundays for their fresh donuts! It is worth the wake-up and the walk.

5.2.6 *The Wayside*

Right on the border of Montpelier and Berlin is the Vermont-famous Wayside Restaurant. I grew up not far from the Wayside, and my parents took us here for breakfast almost every weekend for many years. (My brother infamously would only eat peanut butter for years when we went there. We like to remind him of that now that he's a 6'3" Marine and Brazilian Jiu-Jitsu black belt.) When I moved back to Montpelier, the Wayside continued to be a weekend breakfast tradition for my own family. This is your classic diner and a popular spot for breakfast, especially on the weekend, serving breakfast all day, every day; Sundays, they add Eggs Benedict to their line-up.

Tip 54: Don't be discouraged if you see a line out the door.

The line usually moves at a quick pace, and you won't wait longer than 10-15 minutes for a table. Turnover is pretty regular, just as you would expect at a good diner.

Want to jump the line?

Tip 55: If there are spots at the counter open, you can walk past the line and sit right down at the counter.

This place is outside of downtown, so you will have to drive there, but it's only a 5–10 minute trip.

5.3 Lunch

5.3.1 Wilaiwan's

The most amazing Thai food is served from a tiny shop on State Street called Wilaiwan's. They have three menu offerings a week and rotate menus every week, so what they are serving this week will not be available next week or possibly the week after. Lunch is served from 11 am-2 pm Monday-Saturday, or until they run out.

Tip 56: Call in or line up early to order.

Some dishes are so popular they run out way before closing time. Spiciness can be more than you expect, so if you're not a fan of your mouth being set on fire, ask if they can make yours mild. Many of the dishes can accommodate that request.

Tip 57: Order the Gwit Diow soup if they have it that week.

Oh my goodness, that broth is to die for, and the roasted pork is so tender!

My daughters have also learned of the magic that is the Gwit Diow, so I will order several and ask for the noodles to be in a separate container so I can put it all together when the girls are home from school; that way, the noodles have not overcooked when we sit down to eat.

When the pandemic hit, they stopped allowing people to sit inside. Instead, they will serve your order in a bowl or on a plate if you ask, and you can sit outside to eat as long as you bring back the dishes. Otherwise, it's brought out in standard take-out containers and utensils.

5.3.2 Buddy's Famous Burgers

The local burger joint is called Buddy's Famous Burgers. Lots of specialty burgers to try, along with chicken sandwiches, hot dogs, chicken tenders, hand-cut fries, and tater tots.

Tip 58: Order the poutine (fries covered in cheese curds and hot gravy).

Buddy's makes a really good gravy, and you can add bacon to your order or have the gravy and cheese curds served over tater tots! Omg. And if you didn't catch this recommendation earlier, Buddy's is also the place to get your milkshake on.

5.3.3 Langdon Street Tavern

For pub-style food in a sports bar-type location, hit up Langdon Street Tavern. Solid across the board in terms of food and drinks, it has something for everyone. They do chicken wings really well and have a bunch of sauce options to meet you and your chicken wing needs. Family-friendly, and there is a pool table in the back.

5.3.4 Hunger Mountain Co-op

Within walking distance - in fact, the bike path runs right beside it - Hunger Mountain Co-op offers plenty of "Whole Foods" style groceries but in a community co-op atmosphere. For lunch, it boasts a hot bar with different themed meals each day, such as tacos, Indian, and Thanksgiving (during the season). No matter the theme, there are always roasted meats and many vegetarian options as well. Hunger Mountain Co-op also has a well-stocked salad bar and 3-4 locally-made daily soups. There is also a full-service deli counter with made-to-order sandwiches. I like the Rachel sandwich, and the Muffuletta especially.

Tip 59: Plan a picnic and pick up your supplies from the co-op.

The whole deli area is a section of grab-and-go foods you can easily pack, along with drinks, desserts, and compostable utensils.

5.3.5 Mad Taco

House-smoked meats. Hand-crafted hot sauces. A dedication to inspired Latin cuisine and local beers. This is a high-culinary standard, laid-back eatery with flavor packed into every menu item. I particularly like the quesadillas: cheesy, flavorful, hot, and toasty. Wow, this is sounding really good right now. Maybe I'll get some for lunch today...

5.3.6 Skinny Pancake

Skinny Pancake is your place for sweet and savory crêpes. Be warned, though, that the savory ones are often meals in themselves, not small bites. My daughter raves about their french fries; apparently, that is a hot item for the youth.

5.3.7 Enna

Enna is a new sandwich shop on State Street that grows its own microgreens in the window. The sandwiches are elevated, farm-to-table versions of familiar favorites, like a Reuben, a classic roast beef sandwich, a turkey and cheddar sandwich, a bahn-mi, and an Italian grinder, just to name a few off their menu.

5.3.8 North Branch Café

Montpelier's tea and wine café, the food here is just as much of a draw. Besides a rotating menu of soups and salads, their standard menu features several sushi rolls, spring rolls, knish, flatbread, and a variety of desserts.

5.4 Dinner

5.4.1 Sarducci's Restaurant

Sarducci's is classic, delicious Italian fare. The two women co-owners have been in business for over 30 years, and it's an easy win for dinner. Let me give you some of my quick picks:

Best Appetizer: The antipasto plate. Filled with a variety of meats, cheeses, and grilled and pickled vegetables, this can be a dinner in itself if you want a lot of things to taste and try together. Runner up: Calamari, or the Bruschetta with pesto, tomato, and mozzarella. I would, and have, eaten these as my dinner and been very happy.

Best Salad Dressing: Creamy Italian (if you like cream) and Balsamic Vinaigrette (if you don't want cream). These are made in-house and are so good that some people (cough, cough, me) order a container to bring home.

Best pasta: If you're vegan or vegetarian, the Penne Pugliese is great. They cook the pasta in their vegetable broth, bringing out rich flavor in a meatless dish. My next recommendation for those who embrace meat would be the Bolognese. Balanced and comforting!

Best entree: For comfort, I opt for their chicken parmesan. For seafood, I like the Scampi e Capesante with lightly breaded shrimp and scallops with a buttery lemon garlic linguine.

Best dessert: This is tied between the lemon cream cake and the tiramisu. You can't go wrong with either.

Tip 60: Make your reservations early or arrive early.

It gets busy fast on Friday and Saturday evenings, and during our tourist seasons, it can be packed with a wait list for hours, even on a Wednesday!

Tip 61: Go before 6 pm for better parking spots.

Parking at Sarducci's becomes more of a walk for you if you go later than 6 pm. In the summer, you might not care as much because it's a nice time of the year for a walk, but in winter, you're probably going to care more because a dark, cold walk in the slush and snow is not how you want to begin or end your lovely dinner.

Tip 62: Use the bank parking spaces after 5:30 pm.

After 5:30 pm and over the weekend, you can park in the bank parking spaces and the ones that say Tenant Only across from Sarducci's spaces. Those are all for businesses that close by 5:30 pm. If all of those are taken already, keep driving down the one-way road to find more spots. If it's after 5:30 pm, you also don't have to worry about paying for parking down the road where the ParkMobile app zones are.

5.4.2 Three Penny Taproom

Besides being a top-notch taproom full of a wide range of local craft brews, Three Penny Taproom also offers excellent food to pair with your drinks. Think pub food meets farm-to-table quality.

Tip 63: Try the TPT Burger!

This burger used to be sold only on Friday, and people flocked there to taste the sensation or have more of what they had learned to love! What makes it so special? It's the pickled jalapeños and the peanut butter. Yep. Apparently, that's a great combination that the more culinary-adventurous are rewarded for trying. Get it with the

TPT fries, topped with their Three Penny sauce, a creamy, tangy sauce rich with caramelized onions.

5.4.3 *Positive Pie*

New York-style pizza in Vermont? We have that! Positive Pie, located on State Street, offers slices from the back entrance of the restaurant (located through a narrow connecting road/alleyway off Main Street) and full restaurant fare on the State Street side. In the summer, there is also outdoor seating. Now, I know it's not the exact same as the pie you get in a shop in New York, but my Brooklyn-born dad attests that it's a really good stand-in when he misses home. My favorite is the BBQ chicken pizza, with a BBQ base, red onion, blue cheese crumbles, roasted chicken, and a drizzle of balsamic reduction on top of the mozzarella.

This pizza place is not just good at its specialty; they also have excellent sandwiches, appetizers, and entrees, so everyone in your party will find something they will enjoy. I find their wraps to be my favorite because they use pizza dough to make the wrap, which gives your sandwich this wonderful, warm, pillowy softness.

5.4.4 *Hippie Chickpea*

Located at a brightly-colored hole in the wall on Elm Street, this small place survived the pandemic by offering take-out only and has kept up with that business model. I devour their chicken gyros in a saucy, delicious mess, and my best friend loves their falafel. This place is a pick-up window with some newly installed outdoor seating! You can call ahead or order at the window.

5.4.5 Hugo's Bar and Grill

A new favorite spot in town, serving a one-page menu of fabulous food, ranging from Asian summer rolls and dumplings to bistro burgers and steak frites, everyone at your table will find something to enjoy.

Tip 64: Head downstairs to the grotto bar.

Tucked away from the bustle and din of the upstairs dining room, this slick, wood-topped basement bar, surrounded by the old stone foundation, has been a hidden gem for years.

My friend Helen has encouraged the bartender to stock a Bartender Bibliotherapy library. To help him get started on her mission to open up this mini-library, she and I brought him books with post-it notes to indicate for what conditions he should prescribe them. Since the owner of Hugo's is the President Emeritus of Vermont College of Fine Arts, she assumed he would be cool with his bartender having his own library.

Chapter Review

- Breakfast at the Wayside is a classic diner experience. Lines move quickly, and there is no wait for open seats at the counter.

- On Sundays, Birchgrove Bakery makes fresh donuts so good they make it worth the early wake-up to score a place in line for them.

- Wiliawan's offers three incredible Thai dishes each week from 11 am-2 pm or whenever they sell out. Lines form early.

- Get your picnic supplies from Hunger Mountain Co-op. Great deli case, sandwich station, hot bar, and salad bar.

- Sarducci's is extremely popular and therefore gets busy early. Make reservations ahead of time, or show up before 5:30 pm.

- Three Penny Taproom has its unique TPT Burger that should be on every culinary adventurer's list.

- Hugo's Bar and Grill has delicious food and a bar in the basement to get a good drink and a book to read from the bartender.

Chapter 6: Shopping

6.1 Overview

Montpelier has so much to offer when it comes to shopping. Whether you're looking for gifts to bring home or something special for yourself, it will be hard not to find something, if not several things, you didn't even realize you wanted.

6.2 Small Town Classics

6.2.1 Capitol Stationers

This was my favorite store in Montpelier when I was a kid. Full of colorful pens of different widths and tips and all sorts of sized notebooks to choose from to use those pens, I was obsessed with Capitol Stationers.

Today, I think this is one of the top shops to hit for classic Vermont-themed souvenirs. T-shirts with maple trees that say "I'd Tap That," hand-knit mittens, Eat More Kale shirts (from the famous feud between our hometown artist and Chick-Fil-A), maple cookies and candy, keychains with moose, and so many other novelties.

This is also the store for gift-wrapping options, cards, picture frames, balloons, and of course, notebooks and pens.

6.2.2 Bear Pond Books

A good small town will always have at least one bookstore. We have two!

Bear Pond Books has been in town since 1973. Even after moving locations from across the street, the old wooden floorboards still creak as you walk between the hardwood shelves. Upstairs is a cozy children's area with a resident tortoise and a little playhouse. Besides children's books, this area also has Young Adult novels and graphic novels. Local authors are on display when possible.

If you see books by authors Dan & Jason, they are Montpelier High School graduates. Dan and I went to school together, and his daughters are in my Kids Brazilian Jiu-Jitsu class.

6.2.3 The Book Garden

The other bookstore in town is a tiny shop on State Street. Besides curating a collection of interesting books about Vermont, the occult, nature, foraging, graphic novels, and comic books, the Book Garden also has an extensive section of role-playing games, cards, and figurines.

6.2.4 Woodbury Mountain Toys

Not every small town has a toy store, but every small town should. This is one of the biggest little toy stores I have been in. Its narrow hall of space is literally packed floor-to-ceiling with eye-catching options to entertain babies, toddlers, school-age kids, and even adults like me who still want to play with brain teaser puzzles and Pusheen the Cat.

The common sight here on a Saturday morning is a slew of parents with their kids, finding birthday gifts for the party that starts in a few hours. I know this because I have definitely been that parent and seen other party-goers at the store shopping for the same birthday kid. This is great, actually, because then you are assured you won't get the same gift as them.

Tip 65: Look up!

There is so much to look at in Woodbury Mountain Toys that it is easy to forget to look up and see everything hanging from the ceiling! I especially bring this to your attention if you like to dress up because they have the coolest helmets, hats, and other dress-up head adornments hanging there.

6.2.5 Delish

Small-town candy stores can range from chocolate makers (we used to have one of those) to soda fountains with old-fashioned penny candy displays (we used to have one of those too). Delish is a candy store about the size of my first rented room at college, which was roughly the dimensions of a small walk-in closet, but it offers a little bit of everything. JellyBelly flavors, penny candy, bulk candy, Vermont-made candy, maple candy, holiday-themed candy, PEZ, old-fashioned Bit-O-Honey, Zagnat, Turkish Taffy, and Charleston Chews, and a display case of all kinds of fancy chocolates and truffles.

6.2.6 Aubuchon's Hardware

Finally, what small town would be complete without the local hardware store. Aubuchon's Hardware is everything you expect: knowledgeable, friendly staff, many of whom have been there for years; hardware and painting supplies for anything you may need to build or fix; pet supplies; sleds in the winter; and a couple "store cats" that wander around on their own accord.

6.3 Antiques

6.3.1 J. Langdon

Appropriately situated on Langdon Street, this is a cool shop with a lot of antique furniture, as well as old photographs, home decor, and a case of smaller, delicate, and precious items.

6.3.2 *Antiques*

This small antique shop on Main Street hosts smaller home decor antiques, books, and photographs. While J. Langdon has the room to display big things to capture your attention, this shop is all about the details. Shelves upon shelves of interesting finds wait for your eyes to settle on them out of all the other objects begging for your attention.

6.4 *Clothing and Gear*

6.4.1 *Bailey Road*

Bailey Road is a women's fashion boutique. High-quality wardrobe staples, as well as unique pieces to stand out from the crowd. They just recently expanded from women's clothing into upscale home decor and furnishings. Each display area tells a story of what you might be interested in. Here is the counter of a country kitchen with lemon-scented hand soap, tea towels, and hand-crafted cups and dishes. Here is the living area you want to sit down in with a hot tea or a glass of wine and read your book, with charming throw pillows and hand-poured, scented soy candles. Here is the vanity mirror with jewelry trees and trays filled with silver and gold hand-hammered pendants, earrings, and bracelets, waiting to bring some glimmer to your ensemble. That is just the preview. If you want to see the rest of the home, the door is open.

6.4.2 *Onion River Outdoors*

This is the store for the outdoor enthusiast. Onion River Outdoors specializes in bikes but also has a great range of outdoor gear for camping, hiking, and skiing. Half of the store is gear; the other half is casual athletic clothing like Patagonia and Prana, as well as biking attire.

6.4.3 Roam

Right next door to Onion River Outdoors is Roam, which has mainly women's clothing and shoes. I have to say, though, that the men's section is quite decent, and from what I've heard about male shopping habits, most men would probably find the size adequate for their shopping needs. Along with Patagonia and Prana, this store also stocks Carve, Z Supply, Birkenstock, Dansko, and Smartwool and Darn Tough socks.

Tip 66: Invest in Darn Tough socks!

I'm using the word "invest" here very deliberately because once you buy a pair, you essentially have a pair for life. Darn Tough, made here in Vermont, will replace your socks if you ever wear a hole through them. So upfront, you are spending some dough on a pair of socks, but they are soft, warm, fit great, and breathe well, but you will wear them so much you will eventually wear them out. Then you just mail them to Darn Tough with a form, and they send you a new pair of that style and size. I have done this 5-6 times now, as I turned over my winter sock collection to exclusively Darn Tough. I'm wearing some right now, as a matter of fact.

6.4.4 Salaam Boutique

Salaam Boutique is a women-owned and run business, with all clothes cut and sewn in the USA. The fabrics are luxuriously soft, and the prints are mesmerizing. Check out their storefront on State Street to be drawn into their laid-back, comfortable styles.

6.4.5 Rebel Heart

This store is a fun mix of delights. Fashionable cuts of women's denim, current fits, and trends in tops meet a mystical apothecary and botanical shop. Potted house plants, candles and incense, tarot, paper goods, oils, and accessories are just some of the interesting finds at Rebel Heart.

6.5 Unique Finds

6.5.1 Splash

Another store that takes a few walks around to possibly take in all of the things they have stocked, Splash is the go-to shop for cruelty-free, vegan soaps, haircare, and make-up. They also have a lot of clothing options as well, from comfortable, stretchy undergarments, to slippers, to sweaters, leggings, and skirts.

6.5.2 Cool Jewels

A jewelry-makers delight, Cool Jewels has everything you need to make your own, or you can peruse all of their already-made necklaces, bracelets, and earrings. Filled with all sorts of gems, carved stones, and blown glass, this is a fun wonderland of baubles that will catch your eye everywhere you look.

Tip 67: Take your kids in for the giant box of unsorted, random beads.

It's like an 8-inch-deep sandbox of thousands and thousands of random beads. My youngest daughter loves to plunge her hand in and move it through the beads while she watches different colored and shaped beads come up from the depths. It is a tactile and visual experience and will help keep your well-behaved kid entertained while you look around.

6.5.3 Katie's Jewels

Right next to Cool Jewels is Katie's Jewels, which caters to shoppers looking for sleek, artisan jewelry made with sterling silver, gold, and precious gems.

6.5.4 The Artisan's Hand

This store is a great find for high-end, Vermont-made artisan goods. Blown glass, wooden cutting boards and bowls, glazed, colorful pottery, scarves, framed photography and prints, and cases of jewelry are just some of the most immediate examples of their wares.

6.5.5 Rabble Rouser

Rabble Rouser is an employee-owned and operated café is famous for their Nutty Steph's granola, made a chocolate bar dedicated to our Senator Bernie Sanders, and also gets a mention for the local artists and artisans they support around the café. Books, stickers, ceramics, prints, and jewelry are sold to support local artists.

Tip 68: Rent your gear!

Onion River Outdoors offers rentals that fit the season: mountain bikes, fat bikes, e-bikes, snowshoes, ice skates, backcountry skis, telemark skis, and split boards. If you don't want to pack your outdoor gear, Onion River Outdoors has you covered. Make sure to call ahead for availability, as this service is quite popular with visitors and locals alike.

6.5.6 *Capital Kitchen*

This shop will easily catch your eye as you walk down State Street. Always color-coordinated and themed, you are drawn in by the vibrancy of the design, and then you stay to look at all the items they used to create the tableau of kitchenware.

Tip 69: Get yourself a Jetz-Scrubz.

These are the best scrub sponges I have ever found, and I always buy them from Capital Kitchen. The scrub side scours off hardened food and cleans up all the messes, the soft side cleans your glassware and delicates, and it dries quickly, so you don't feel like it's growing an army of bacteria next to your sink. (And when it's getting old, it turns into the scrubber I use for sinks and bathrooms and continues to power through every job.) Even the owner agrees that these are *the best* scrubber sponges ever.

I also love Capital Kitchen's selection of reusable items for lunches and drinks, as well as their always dazzling assortment of printed bowls. I no longer have matching bowls at home, but I do have an array of interesting, colorful bowls that makes me love them again every time I go to use them.

6.5.7 *Buch Spieler*

"Vermont's independent record store since 1973." Tucked in on Langdon Street since they opened, Buch Spieler continues to offer curated current musical selections and vinyl.

6.5.8 *AroMed*

Connected to Capital Cannabis, AroMed sells CBD products, as well as ointments, salves, and other holistic creations to support your wellness. They also have diffusers and incense for aromatherapy, crystals and candles for balance and energy work, and a large array of essential oils.

Tip 70: Try the Calm-Aid oil and Arnica patches.

Years ago, my massage therapist recommended the Calm-Aid oil blend sold at AroMed, and I have been hooked since. I'm not the only fan either because this oil is frequently almost sold out or is sold out completely. My other favorite at AroMed is the Natural Patches of Vermont Arnica patches you can put on your sore muscles to help heat and relax them. Training in Brazilian Jiu-Jitsu, I have used these patches for years.

Chapter Review

- Main Street and State Street make up around 90% of the local shopping downtown.

- Langdon Street has the other 10%.

- Darn Tough socks are a worthwhile investment you can purchase at Roam or Onion River Outdoors.

- Support an employee-owned business and reproductive justice at Rabble Rouser by buying chocolate vulvas.

- Capitol Stationers is a great place for traditional Vermont souvenirs.

- The Artisan's Hand is the shop for hand-crafted items you will want to display in your home or give as a meaningful gift to someone special.

Chapter 7 Blend in like a Local

7.1 Overview

Why do you travel? If you're like most people, you travel to see things you may not get to experience at home. It may be new cuisine that incites your interest, geological formations and natural environment that your part of the world does not have, or the way other people live that is different from you.

One way to experience a new culture is to immerse yourself in its ways. Learning the language, trying on the attitude, and basically living like a local. This chapter is for those who would like to take a break from their way of life and try small-town Montpelier living for a change.

7.2 Attitude is Everything

7.2.1 Small Town Manners Matter

I used to live in Boston, where the standard greeting of a stranger was to stare straight ahead and pretend they didn't exist, but Montpelier works differently. This is a community of neighbors, so we live within the understanding that just because you don't know someone directly doesn't mean they don't know you or know about you. So if you're a jerk to a stranger, it's very possible that the stranger knows your neighbor, your co-worker, or your child's teacher.

Tip 71: Be friendly.

One summer, I was at a stoplight where I knew that when the cars in the left-turn lanes got their green light, there was a split-second to turn right from my lane before I would be in their way. This particular time, I opted not to rush because I had my family in the car with me. As I sat patiently to let the left-turning cars go first, I heard a man's voice from the car next to me tell me, "Hey, you know you can go right on red there." Now, my first inclination was to whip around and tell this know-it-all where to go because I know I can go right on red, and I don't need you - guy sitting in the passenger seat of another car - to tell me how to drive. But I reminded myself that this person might not know I know all about this, and I should probably not mouth off to him until I verify he's a jerk. So I turned to look at the guy, and as I started to explain how I didn't want to cut off the left-turning cars, which I know from experience is annoying as heck, I realized that 1) I was talking to the Chief of Police, and 2) his wife, who was driving, was my son's 6th-grade teacher, who by the way, also knew me because her son was one of my classmates in school.

We all had a good laugh waving and saying hello once everyone recognized each other, but that was proof enough for me that being kind is always the best first response.

This brings me naturally to my next point. Not only was I kind in the above scenario, but I was also demonstrating another important attitude to foster here.

Tip 72: Be patient.

This applies everywhere: at stores, while driving, and even at the crosswalks. You know how I can always tell someone is from out of town? Because they jump the signaled crosswalks. They don't know the traffic patterns, and in many cities, jaywalking is an unwritten right. To an outsider, the lighted intersection at State and Main seems exceptionally slow because it doesn't let opposing traffic off State Street go at the same time. Each light from the State Street directions has its own, separately-timed green lights, so if you are at the intersection of State and Main, and it seems like no one has a greenlight and you are thinking of jumping the crosswalk signal, please, be patient. Don't walk out in front of my car thinking all is clear when my light turns green. I don't have a lot of time to get through this light, and I am already talking to you while in my car, encouraging you to stay on the sidewalk and wait because I can see you looking around, wondering if you can jump the signal safely. I won't run you over if you do walk in front of me during my 3-second light, but rest assured, I am saying some nasty things about *your* impatience while you visit *my* town.

As you can see from our kindness and patience, we try to be thoughtful about how we impact those in our community. So to complete today's lesson on small-town etiquette in Montpelier, here is a final tip:

Tip 73: Don't smoke around others if you can help it.

I'm not saying you can't smoke - no one here is going to implicitly infringe on your freedom to light up unless you're next to a state building or a school - but smoking while walking down the sidewalk is rare here. So rare that I assume that when I do see this downtown, I'm certain they must be from another state. Local people who smoke seem to do so next to a smoking receptacle and have generally stepped away from people walking by. No one is shamed for smoking; this is just considerate of others in town. Be kind by not making others breathe in your smoke; be patient and find a place to smoke that least disturbs others making their way around town.

7.2.2 Caring for the Environment Everyday

Our community has come together on several environmental impact issues, so part of learning to live the Montpelier life is embracing how you can do small things for the environment.

Tip 74: Bring or purchase a reusable bag.

First, we got rid of plastic bags used in stores in Montpelier to reduce the reliance on a product that does not break down easily, pollutes our environment, and hurts our wildlife. Then, we reduced our impact on trees by eliminating free paper bags and encouraging people to use reusable shopping bags instead. Let me tell you, reusable shopping bags are so much better than their plastic and paper counterparts: you can stuff so much more in them without that nagging fear that the material might break. I use mine not only for casual shopping and groceries but when I need to throw things together for a picnic or a beach day or one of my girls is going to a sleepover. Those reusable shopping bags work well and look good too. If you don't have one, head to Capitol Stationers on Main

Street. They have a good selection of strong and small nylon bags that can fit in your pocket and more substantial, Vermont-themed canvas bags, which is a great way to passive-aggressively brag to your friends back home about where you were last weekend.

Tip 75: Bring your own water bottle or coffee mug.

The theme here is reducing plastic and paper waste. Maybe your part of the country isn't there yet, but you can bring back some Montpelier, Vermont attitude by returning with a water bottle and toting your hydration everywhere you go. Not only is it better for Nalgene or Hydro Flask the environment, but you will be more likely to drink water during the day when it is easily accessible in a swank container. And I will tell you what I tell my daughters and everyone who will listen, "We all need to be drinking more water!" You've got a headache? Drink some water. Your muscles are sore? Drink some water. Your skin is dry? Drink some water. Whatever ails you, it would probably help to drink some water.

Tip 76: Get ready for the compostable straws.

Remember those horrible videos of turtles choking on plastic straws and the calls for 'Save the Turtles' across the Internet? Montpelier heeded the call and changed their straw strategy. You will find that some places have changed to corn-based compostable straws, some have switched to hardened paper straws, and some offer no straws at all anymore. If you want the extra bonus Montpelier points, purchase a metal straw that can go everywhere with you. I personally find metal straws make drinking cold drinks more enjoyable.

After you have packed your reusable bag with your Montpelier purchases, filled your reusable bottle with fresh, cold water, and are enjoying your iced tea with a metal straw, make sure to do your part to throw trash and recycling into their designated waste bins. We try to recycle as much as possible around here, and some places will even have a compost bucket for food scraps. We are serious about our impact on the environment, and when you're here playing Blend in With the Locals, you should be serious too.

7.3 *Look the Part*

Whenever I travel, I play a little game in my head called "Look Like I Live Here," and the goal is to figure out how the locals dress so I can attempt to pass as one. For example, if I visit a city, especially in the Northeast, I wear even more black than I currently sport because I know that black is more commonly worn in cities and always looks good. If I go somewhere warm and beachy, I wear more color and light, flowy fabrics, even though I would never generally choose color or flowy fabrics in my everyday life. So if you're like me and also like to play this game, let me give you a head start on looking like you live here.

7.3.1 *Clothing Staples*

Tip 77: Wear a flannel shirt.

Look "Vermont" immediately with a flannel shirt. In fact, we have our own company appropriately named the Vermont Flannel Company. But even off-brand flannel will suffice to help you blend in. Plaids are best. The ultra-Vermonter plaid is the Buffalo, red and black checked plaid, but other plaids are acceptable and will not raise suspicion.

Tip 78: Wear your comfortable shoes.

I will preface this explanation with: Yes, locals may wear nice shoes, shiny leather, or high heels *when the weather is good*. But those fancy fancies will get ruined in the salt and sand-laden plowed sidewalks or the heavy rain, and since our 6-months of winterish weather combines the two, most locals rarely wear the fancy stuff. In the summer, basic sandals blend in everywhere, but in the cooler months, what you will see on a local is a shoe that is comfortable or a straight-up winter boot or hiking boot.

7.3.2 Be Prepared for the Weather

So you know about the appropriate footwear for Vermont. What else can you do to prepare for the weather here?

Tip 79: Wear layers.

We have a saying in Vermont: "If you don't like the weather, just wait 10 minutes." The warm breeze can become a cold chill when the sun is blocked by a cloud. A warm spring day can feel very cold when the breeze skirts along the melting ice and snow and hits you in your t-shirt. And in winter, all those jackets and sweaters can build up heat as you trudge through fresh snow, making you desperate to get more cold air on your skin. So we all wear layers. That's also a great use for your flannel.

Tip 80: Wear a down-insulated jacket in winter.

The last time I was downtown in the winter, I paid attention to the similarities of the pedestrians, and there were *so many down-insulated jackets* on display I had to make a note of it for you. Not ski jackets, mind you because that screams tourist to me, but the inner layer under the shell.

What about wool pea coats? That is what a lawyer or a legislator might wear to match his suit. Nothing against them, and not to say we don't own pea coats, but they are on the formal side for this casual town.

Tip 81: Have a winter hat on hand.

Am I the only one who felt uncomfortable during Game of Thrones scenes in the snow where *no one* was wearing a hat? Everyone has the warmest fur coats I've ever seen, and then they top it off -- in the wind and snow -- with *nothing*. This world has magic and dragons, and they have learned how to make incredible potions and explosives, but *no one* has figured out how to knit a winter hat as they march off to fight the Night King?

I debated also suggesting that you carry a scarf or gloves on hand, but I thought that the most reasonable item you might consider would be, at the very least, a hat. Keep your head warm. It makes such a difference, and especially if you are traveling with children, keeping them happy and warm when it cools off is going to make your whole trip with them better.

Chapter Review

- Be friendly - everyone knows everyone around here.

- Be patient - unless you're saving a life, there's no need to rush. Especially at lights and crosswalks.

- Be considerate of others and second-hand smoke. If your choice is negatively impacting someone else, please make your choice elsewhere.

- Invest in the environment by bringing or purchasing reusables: shopping bags, water bottles, travel mugs, and bonus points for a metal straw.

- Dress for the weather, especially in winter: layers, insulated jackets, and a hat!

Chapter 8: Hubbard Park

8.1 Overview

Designated in 1899, Hubbard Park is a central feature of
Montpelier. In fact, the woods you see behind the Capitol building?
That is all Hubbard Park. It wraps around the hillside, stretching
behind homes all the way over to where the woods meet Elm Street
and down towards the Rec Fields and the North Branch Nature
Center.

8.2 Top Spots

8.2.1 The Tower

The Tower is a 52-foot-tall stone structure at the highest point of
the park and is an immediate draw to visitors and residents alike.
It's a great place to stop and have lunch and is always a draw for
kids. Not only do they want to see the top, but the hollow inside is
very echoey, and kids love to hear their voices bounce off the sides
of the interior.

**Tip 82: Take the metal staircase leading to the top, where
you can get a great view of the mountains surrounding
Montpelier.**

Don't worry, the top of the tower has a 4-foot-tall wall to prevent
falls, and the wall itself is two feet thick. It also includes a little
bench for those whose legs are burning after the march up the
steps.

When the park was first dedicated, much planning took place to
create an experience that would fit the needs of the town and attract
visitors to use the new paths and picnic areas. The architect selected
for the job suggested a stone tower "observatory," as had been built
in Somerville and Newton, Massachusetts.

The plans were embraced, and an Italian stone mason, John Miglierini, who had emigrated to Montpelier in 1893, was contracted to build the structure. Miglierini and his company had previously worked on the Hubbard Memorial Chapel at Green Mount Cemetery, the Barre firehouse, and projects at Fort Ethan Allen.

Montpelier set aside $500 a year for construction and material costs, so Miglierini and his crew would work for a few weeks every summer on the project until funds dried up for the year. It is thought that he used fieldstone from abandoned stone walls nearby to build the tower and to help keep costs low.

Although the top of the tower looks unfinished, it was built that way on purpose to evoke the feeling of a medieval tower ruin.

After 14 years of steady construction, the tower was first opened to the public in 1930. Miglierini died the same year and is buried in the Green Mount Cemetery.

8.2.2 Composting Toilets

There are toilets available in the park, but they are composting toilets, so here's what to expect. The toilets are located in very sturdy, comfortable outhouses. Inside you will see two seats for toilets. One will have a bucket of sawdust on it or will be closed another way. The other will be available to use. If your waste is solid, throw a cup or two of sawdust down after, then close the lid. As you leave, close the latch on the door -- this keeps squirrels, chipmunks, and other creatures out of the outhouse, which would be an unenjoyable surprise for most people in need of a bathroom in the middle of the woods.

8.2.3 The Fitness Trail

When I was a kid in the 80s, they took everyone in my class into Hubbard Park to use the newly christened Fitness Trail. Our teachers handed out a checklist of fitness structures we were supposed to use appropriately so we could check them off as we walked along. I remember feeling confused by these metal pole and wooden beam constructions because even with a sign posted at each one with instructions on what it was and how to use it, and a totally 80s-styled kid pictured to encourage us to use it correctly, I still did not get how this led to fitness.

We ended up improvising on how one should use these man-made elements in the woods. Metal poles are always for hanging and swinging on. Wooden planks or beams are for jumping on and off or climbing. Take your kids and see if they do anything different. They won't. There is a natural order to the use of this fitness trail, and no sign or checklist will change humans' instinctive tendencies.

Tip 83: Find the Monkey Bars made for giants.

I'm not sure who they had in mind when they created this particular structure, but there are only a handful of people in the world who can use these Monkey Bars. Even if you haul yourself three feet up the rungs of the metal ladder, you have to be almost six feet tall to reach the bars overhead. Good luck.

During the pandemic, my two closest friends from grade school and I became a Pandemic Pod and would hike around Montpelier early every Sunday morning. As we walked the Fitness Trail portion of Hubbard Park, we always noted one particular structure that always stood out as more ominous than playful. I think one is supposed to do sit-ups on it, but the way the wooden plank is angled, we all agreed it seemed like a set-up for waterboarding someone. Or it's a really lame slide. Whatever its real job is, I'm pretty sure no one uses it for that.

8.2.4 The View from Cliff Street

Cliff Street is named very appropriately, as the road and houses that run alongside are perched precariously along the cliff above Elm Street. The sign on the street says it is a 16% grade, which doesn't sound like a whole lot until you try walking up that way into the park.

Tip 84: Walk down Cliff Street from the park and enjoy the amazing view of Montpelier all the way down the street.

At several stops, you will find yourself overlooking the town in new ways -- seeing the tops of homes, buildings, and churches and the little connecting roads weaving through neighborhoods and heading out of town. Some of the best pictures of Montpelier are taken from locations on Cliff Street.

Tip 85: Take your pictures from Cliff Street at night, in the winter.

Some of the best-published pictures of Montpelier are taken from those Cliff Street locations, and the little lights of the town against the dark backdrop of our natural environment make for beautiful photos. Winter, where white snow contrasts with the darkness and reflects the lights in town, is the ultimate beauty.

8.3 Dogs in the Parks

8.3.1 Current Leash Law

From the City of Montpelier:

Hubbard Park:

- Dogs are welcome in Hubbard Park and may be off-leash

- Make sure your dog is either on a leash or under voice control at all times, as required by City Ordinance

- Always keep your dog in sight

- Don't allow your dog to approach people or other dogs without mutual agreement

- Don't assume others want to interact with your dog

- Carry a leash for each dog you walk, and be prepared to leash your dog as needed

- Dog owners must pick up after their dogs. Use receptacles provided or carry out

- Dogs must have a current rabies vaccine

North Branch River Park:

- Dogs are welcome in North Branch River Park and must be on a leash at all times (City Ordinance requires dogs to be either leashed or under voice control at all times)

- Don't allow your dog to approach people or other dogs without mutual agreement

- Don't assume others want to interact with your dog

- Dog owners must pick up after their dogs. Use receptacles provided or carry out

- Dogs must have a current rabies vaccine

I know you want your dog to be one of those pups that join you on your hike and stay by your side the whole time, so you might be motivated to remove the leash and assume that how your dog listens to you at home will be the same in the park. Let's assume 100% of the people who let their dog run off the leash feel this way. Out of that 100% of people, my experience is that only 3-5% of people actually have any real control over their dogs as they walk, trot, or tear down the trails at breakneck speeds.

Not everyone loves dogs as much as you do, especially small children who get bombarded with a dog right in their face or see this child-sized beast running straight for them. It's scary for them. I had to step in front of my kids when they were little to give them some physical protection as someone's well-meaning but obnoxiously-mannered dog came running at us to say 'hi.' I love dogs. But I love my kids more, and no one is impressed with your lack of control.

Tip 86: Keep your dog on a leash unless it has amazing recall skills the moment you call them. Anything lower than that standard requires a leash.

No one should be made to feel uncomfortable in the park, even if you personally happen to feel super comfy with strange dogs coming at you. And no one should feel entitled to treat the park as they please at the expense of others' enjoyment.

My best friend has even started reminding people of the leash law when she gets accosted on her runs. And we love dogs so much! But if you clearly don't have your dog under your immediate control, she will let you know of your lack of consideration of others using the park as she runs past you. You have been warned.

8.3.2 The Dog Park

There is, however, an area of the park next to the third parking lot area as you drive in the main entrance, which is an unofficial dog park. Owners will let their well-trained dogs off-leash here to run around with other dogs. But please be aware that this area is still part of the main hiking area for people without dogs, and not everyone enjoys a dog speeding at full tilt at them or their children, so you are still expected to have excellent verbal control over your dog if you choose to let them run around here.

8.3.3 *What to Do If You Lose Your Dog*

Full of smells and textures and wild animals, your dog may lose their sense of obedience (if it had much to begin with) and wander off into the park. This is where your small-town connections and manners are your lifeline.

First, as you walk the trails looking and calling for your dog, you can ask anyone you come across whether they have seen your dog. People pay attention to dogs without owners, and someone may have seen yours, and they may even try to help you find it.

I found a dog in the middle of the park once with my daughters, and when it became clear that this little pup was not with any owner, we got close enough to put it on a makeshift leash using headphone wires. The tag said "Greta" and had a phone number, but the owner (who turned out to be a friend of several of my book club members) did not pick up.

This brings us to the second move if you can't find your dog in the park, check with the local police station. Many lost dogs are brought there as a central drop-off point, and the police will continue to try to find the owner. When I brought Greta there, they had Greta's photo up on their Facebook page within minutes.

And what happened to Greta? Her owner eventually called me back after hearing my message. Apparently, she had gone home during her lunch break to let Greta out, and Greta decided to take a lunch break of her own into the park! I let her know where I had brought her dog, and she and Greta were reunited that afternoon.

8.4 *Events in the Park*

Since Hubbard Park is so closely and conveniently located in Montpelier, it is a great site for several fun official and unofficial events during the year.

8.4.1 The Enchanted Forest

Tip 87: If you visit near Halloween, look up Haunted Forest tickets.

Every year, local volunteers carve hundreds of pumpkins and place them around a main trail in the park. Then, people with tickets are treated to a wagon ride through the forest, listening to ghost stories along the way, all while sight-seeing all these amazing, glowing faces. If you don't have tickets, don't worry, you can still walk the lit-up trails after the wagon rides are over for the evening. But if you want tickets, buy them early through the City Clerk's Office at City Hall. They sell out fast.

8.4.2 Parkapalooza

In the summer, Hubbard Park hosts Parkapalooza, which uses Hubbard Park as a gathering place for live concerts. Using a stage made from natural materials, these free concerts are put on in the early evening, usually on a weekday. If weather permits, there is sometimes a 100-foot-long slip-and-slide! While free to the public, donations are welcome, and this event is generally a carry-in-carry-out situation. This is a great opportunity to go to the Hunger Mountain Co-op, pick up picnic supplies for the show, tote them in your reusable bag, and blend in with the community.

8.4.3 Killer Hill

After you enter the park through the main entrance, you will notice a very steep hill on your right with a shelter located at the top. This hill is where everyone goes sliding (or sledding, depending on where you're from) in the winter. I'm not sure if it still goes by the same moniker we used when I was a kid, but we called it Killer Hill. It sounded death-defying and, therefore, very cool, and it denoted the bit of the risk to your life you felt when you bombed down the hill in your cheap little plastic sled. It may have been the cheapest thing your parents could get, but those little plastic sleds are makeshift rockets on packed snow.

First, the speed you can accumulate on your way down the hill can feel like death is imminent, and most of us will find our survival instincts kicking in as we try to slow our plastic death machine with our hands. But unfortunately, that's when we learn that that method doesn't work well.

Second, as you near the end of the hill at speeds well beyond what God intended for you in a sled, you realize that after the hill is simply the road. Now, the park's staff wisely built a boundary hill here to help people slow down before launching themselves into the road, and for the most part, this works. But for those whose self-preservation instincts did not kick in earlier, they will experience some air-time as the boundary wall now becomes a jump essentially, lifting them up and over to meet the road. This is where the fear may finally kick in, but by now, it's too late, and the best anyone can do is bail out mid-air and enjoy a rough landing.

Finally, Killer Hill can also sneak attack you. This comes in the form of natural and man-made bumps, jumps, and divets in the middle of the hill. On a bright, snowy day, you often won't see these challenges until it's too late, at which point your tailbone takes the impact. The older ones of the group then roll out of their sled in pain and wish they hadn't tried to be young again. The youth often just scream as if they are on a rollercoaster and don't seem as physically affected. For them, the risk is losing control or sitting in their sled. They may fall out, and the sled continues the trek without them, or they hold on for dear life and end up continuing their travels backward, sideways, or at least tenuously until they eventually fall out.

Tip 88: Sliding works best on packed snow. You won't go very far if it's thick with light, fluffy snow.

Tip 89: Use a snow tube. It's way better on your backside.

Chapter Review

- Visit the Tower. It's visually impressive, and hiking to the top grants you a unique view of Montpelier and the surrounding mountains.
- The Fitness Trail in Hubbard Park offers playground-esque structures for kids and adults to play on. Feel free to ignore the suggestions on the signs about how to use them.

- Cliff Street is one of the best spots for pictures of Montpelier.

- Be aware and respectful of the dog leash laws in Montpelier, especially in the parks. If you don't have 100% verbal control over your dog in public, it should be on a leash.

- If you bring your kids in the winter, run down some of their energy sliding down Killer Hill. Pick up cheap plastic sleds at Aubuchon's Hardware if you have a slight death wish, or splurge on a comfy snow tube.

- Sliding in the winter is only fast and fun when the snow is packed down. Fresh powder is usually pretty slow.

Chapter 9 Montpelier and the Arts

9.1 Overview

Outdoor activities and the arts stand out in Montpelier. There are so many talented folks in the immediate area that it only makes sense to use their works to beautify and enhance the town.

9.2 ArtWalk Friday

Art Friday is the first Friday of every month when local galleries and shops open up for free to allow the public to enjoy local artwork.

Tip 90: Get the most out of Art Friday by using the Gallery Map. www.montpelieralive.com/artwalk

This map points out all the hidden gems of galleries quietly interspersed amongst the shops, cafés, and restaurants.

Tip 91: Enjoy Art Friday by stopping at local bars and restaurants along the way.

Visiting all the art stops in Montpelier requires energy, and the best way to keep up your energy is to eat and drink regularly, so why not combine the two? I encourage you to start early in the evening with a small dinner, hit a few galleries on the map, then stop for a drink somewhere close by before continuing on. Many of the bars in town also serve food, so you can get a quick bite and something to sip when you need to refuel for your art walk.

By the end of the night, you will have walked off a lot of your food and drink, maybe hit your 10,000 steps for the day, and have seen a wide array of local art in Montpelier. Win, win, win.

9.3 Galleries

As the Art Walk map may have shown you, there are many art galleries in Montpelier. What follows are just some of the larger examples in town, but please use the Art Walk map to locate and visit all of the venues that showcase our local artists and their works.

9.3.1 The Wood Gallery

Our largest gallery is The Wood Gallery on Barre Street, located in a former Catholic convent and school. Named after the late, famous resident artist, T. W. Wood, this gallery was dedicated in 1895 and has moved around Montpelier several times, from Vermont Mutual Insurance to the second floor of the Kellogg-Hubbard Library, to College Hall on the Vermont College campus, to its current location. It is the home of over 700 works of art by T. W. Wood, along with gifts from his friendships with artist contemporaries, such as Frederick S. Church, Asher B. Durand, William Beard, J. G. Brown, and many others.

Tip 92: Visit the headquarters of the PinBox 3000, home of the award-winning, first cardboard pinball machine!

Located in the same building as The Wood Gallery, owner, and creator Ben Matchstick of the Cardboard Teck Instantute welcomes the public to come by and check out his rotating gallery of uniquely designed cardboard pinball machines made by a range of artists from famous graphic artists to local students.

Ben's business partner, the highly creative Pete Talbot, was a friend of my brothers in school, and both Ben and Pete are very engaging to talk to if you have a chance to meet either of them.

Tip 93: Pick up a PinBox 3000 for yourself or as a gift from Woodbury Mountain Toys.

These sets are also used in schools to teach about design, art, and even STEM topics!

9.3.2 The Front

Located in a small spot on Barre Street, The Front is the type of gallery that embodies progressive values. A cooperative gallery, The Front acknowledges the history of Vermont in taking land from the native Abenaki people and the inequity experienced by marginalized communities and uses their space to educate and address inequity, not only within their community of artists but for the public at large.

9.3.3 Vermont College of Fine Arts

Another gallery can be found at our own Vermont College of Fine Arts at the top of East State Street. The historical fixture of Vermont College in Montpelier is now home to top-rated MFA degree programs in Writing, Graphic Design, Music Composition, and Visual Arts. In addition, curated exhibitions feature the school's artists and rotate throughout the year.

9.3.4 The Artisan's Hand

If you want to buy some beautiful art made by local and other Vermont artists, check out the Artisan's Hand on Main Street. They offer handmade jewelry, textiles, glassware, wooden cutting boards and bowls, prints, and photography.

9.3.5 AroMed

Located on the opposing side of Capitol Cannabis, AroMed often features the works of local artists.

9.3.6 Rabble Rouser

This employee-owned coffee shop/chocolate producer/art space showcases and sells the works of many Vermont artisans. From cards to zines, to jewelry, to pottery, and more, this shop pairs delicious treats with support for local artists.

9.3.7 City Center

The main lobby of City Center, which houses the Artisan's Hand, the Skinny Pancake, and the AT&T store, used to be much more active than it is today. But one element that has not changed is the display of local art along its walls on the first floor. Sometimes accompanied by poetry during PoemCity in April, the art of local students is often showcased, as well as other local artists throughout the year.

9.3.8 The Statehouse Cafeteria

During legislative sessions, the cafeteria hosts monthly art shows to enjoy while you eat in their modestly priced, locally-sourced establishment. When the legislature is not in session, the cafeteria will keep exhibits available for longer durations.

9.3.9 VT Supreme Court Gallery

Between the State House and the Pavilion sits a stately building that is the Vermont Supreme Court, which, besides hearing and ruling on cases, also hosts a gallery curated with contemporary Vermont artists. These exhibits rotate on a quarterly basis, and over the past 20 years, the Supreme Court Gallery has displayed the works of many of Vermont's best painters, photographers, and installation artists.

9.4 PoemCity

April is National Poetry Month, and in Montpelier, it is celebrated by calling for all citizens to submit works of original poetry to the PoemCity committee. Final works selected by the committee are published in the local newspapers, as well as printed on laminated paper and posted all around town. Literally, all around town, you will find poetry on windows, doors, signposts, shops, restaurants, cafés, government buildings, and offices. PoemCity is everywhere, and the authors range in age from school children to members of the Senior Center and everyone in between.

9.5 Green Mountain Film Festival

Although they were on hiatus during the pandemic, the Green Mountain Film Festival will continue their 23-year annual tradition in 2024, featuring films by local and foreign directors at Montpelier's independent Savoy Theater. Several of my former high school classmates have had their works selected for this gathering of film aficionados.

Tip 94: Get your tickets *early*.

The shows for this festival easily sell out in advance.

Tip 95: Line up for the show early.

The theaters at the Savoy are small, and the lines of people waiting to get in can be long. So after you have secured your tickets in advance, line up early to get the seats you want.

Tip 96: Plan lunch and dinner around the shows.

Restaurants before the shows get packed quickly because everyone wants to eat before they head into the theater. Now that you know that, make your reservations early or arrive at the restaurant you want to eat at early to beat out your film-going compatriots. This will ensure you get out in time to be first in line at the theater with your advance tickets!

Chapter Review

- Artwalk is on the first Friday of the month.

- If you miss the Artwalk, you'll still see a lot of local art displayed in cafés, public buildings, and shops around town.

- The Artisan's Hand is the best place to shop for Vermont-made arts and crafts.

- PoemCity fills the town spaces with poetry from members of the community every April.

- Green Mountain Film Festival is a big draw: get tickets and your place in line early!

Chapter 10: Hauntings

10.1 Overview

Any city with a storied past will likely have some hauntings, and Montpelier is no exception. With connections to the Civil War and dramas over jilted lovers, Montpelier has quite a few ghostly residents and superstitious stories.

10.2 Green Mount Cemetery

Green Mount Cemetery, residing at 250 State Street, along the river drive on the outskirts of town, was dedicated in 1854; the land was purchased by a prominent local lawyer and the town itself. It came into being at a time when city cemeteries, like Montpelier's Elm Street Cemetery, were becoming filled to capacity, and rural cemeteries became more fashionable, as the space on the outskirts of town allowed for conscientious design choices and monuments that would not otherwise fit in the smaller, older lots of the city cemeteries. As a result, Green Mount Cemetery quickly became an example of pastoral beauty for those who have passed on and their families who would visit the graves of loved ones. At the time, unlike our use of the space today, the landscaping, artistic monuments, and green space of rural cemeteries encouraged the public to use the space for non-grieving activities, such as picnics.

There is a 450 square foot Soldiers Lot that was used during the Civil War to inter Union soldiers. The remains of eight Union soldiers are still buried at the western edge of the cemetery.

While the cemetery is filled with local historical figures and families, it is locally well-known for its paranormal activity. Decades upon decades of local lore cite people seeing glowing red eyes over gravestones, hearing footsteps behind them but never seeing anyone, hearing screams, and seeing glowing orbs. But if you want to go to the most haunted graves and challenge their haunted story, here are some of the most well-known occupants and their hauntings.

Tip 97: Older gravestones are concentrated towards the front and the right side of the cemetery, while newer resting places are towards the back and left. The Civil War Soldier's lot is towards the front left of the cemetery.

10.2.1 Black Agnes

One of the very visually impressive monuments in the cemetery is a green, patinated copper statue sitting along a granite bench that oversees the burial tomb underneath. Although it is called Black Agnes, the statue is green and actually depicts a man wrapped in a shroud: Thanatos (Greek for Death).

This grave was erected for John E. Hubbard. This same man also built the chapel and vault for the cemetery, donated money for land for Hubbard Park, and helped build the Kellogg Hubbard Library. Despite the sound of philanthropy, Hubbard was considered to be a stingy man in town. His wealth came from contesting the will of his childless aunt, who had bequeathed her fortune to the town, especially for a public library. Hubbard won his contest, ignored the rights of his siblings to any of the money, and then planned a much smaller library than his aunt had requested in her will. And it wasn't like he didn't have money: the Hubbard family was one of the original clans of Montpelier, his father and grandfather being shrewd businessmen. So claiming his late aunt's fortune and denying the town the grand library she had indicated in her will made him a general persona non grata for many of his remaining years. However, upon his death, he turned his reputation around by bequeathing money for a park, library, chapel, and gates for Green Mount Cemetery.

The pathos of the statue of Black Agnes is considered to reveal Hubbard's anguished soul, and the legend is that if you sit on Black Agnes' lap or tomb at night, especially at midnight and *especially* on a full moon, of course, the spirit that haunts the grave will curse you. The local lore is that three boys sat on the tomb at midnight on a full moon once, daring to chance fate. The boys saw midnight come and go and left without harm. However, within a week, one boy fell and broke his leg, one was in a serious car accident, and the last drowned in the Winooski River after his canoe capsized. By this point in time, no one can verify the truth, but the stories have survived the test of time, as I recall being told the same stories on the playground.

10.2.2 Little Margaret

Backed by a slice of woods stands a statue of a little girl resting against a granite railing. This is "Little Margaret" Pitkin, who died at seven years old from spinal meningitis. Before her death in 1899, she was widely known in Montpelier for her sweet disposition, beauty, and performances in town amateur productions. Her illness was short, just a few days, before she succumbed to the infection, leaving her parents devastated by the sudden loss of their only child.

The lore surrounding this special statue is that her father sent a photograph of his daughter to a monument company and insisted that every detail in the photo be represented in the statue. You can see these details in the eyelet trim of her dress, the ring on her finger, and the pearl necklace she wears. However, when he received the monument, the father initially refused to pay the bill because he pointed out that a button was missing from the little girl's shoe. The sculptor then showed him the photograph showing that one of her little shoes had lost a button.

The haunting of this grave is a counterpoint to John E. Hubbard's writhing Black Agnes legend. While his grave is for a wealthy old man and the haunting borderlines on possible evil, Little Margaret's gravestone is adorned with flowers, and visitors leave pennies or buttons on the monument in exchange for wishes.

The legend I was told when I was a kid was that someone once left a penny amongst the other offerings and came back the next day to find nothing there but the bare monument as if Little Margaret had taken the offering. Now, adult me can rationalize that a caretaker cleaned the monument off, but it's more fun to think that the spiritual world wants those pennies instead.

Tip 98: Bring a penny, button, or some little offering when you visit and make a wish. We can all use any luck we can get.

10.3 Vermont College

The grounds of Vermont College of Fine Arts have a long and storied past. The building of College Hall was the original building on the campus, an example of classic Second French empire architecture. Built in 1872, it was originally Montpelier Seminary before becoming Vermont Junior College in 1941. The location was a high ground in Montpelier, close to the railroad and the Capitol building, and also had some features left over from the Civil War. During the war, the main green had been used for Sloan United Stations Military Hospital, which helped care for wounded soldiers brought by train from battles further south.

So you would think that the haunting of the building would likely come from Civil War ghosts that never made it home from the battlefield, but instead, the haunting of Vermont College is from a murdered woman of a love triangle that made national news in 1897.

10.3.1 The Ghost of Anna Wheeler

The ghost of Anna Wheeler is said to haunt the 4th floor of College Hall, especially the tower. Decades of anecdotal experience tell of objects being moved in offices, doors opening or closing on their own, framed pictures falling off walls in unison, and furniture inside an unused, locked office moved to block the door. The door to the tower is covered in carvings of messages to Anna, and people even bring letters to her, dropping them off at the 4th floors offices of the MFA in Writing program. Employees who work in the building describe the presence as non malevolent and maybe mischievous.

I worked in College Hall for a number of years, and I can attest to the doorway, the stories, and a general acceptance of this ghost. Unfortunately, I cannot attest to any personally witnessed encounters. Still, the building is old and very strangely built, so I can totally buy that some "different" energy finds it enjoyable to live there.

Despite the spirit connection to College Hall, her murder happened a little further off in a meadowy area of an adjacent neighborhood. Folklore says that the last thing Anna saw before she died was the College Hall tower.

The story behind the murder goes like this:

Anna Wheeler, 17, was engaged to Jack Wheeler, 22 (no relation), who lived on Sibley Avenue, which is very close to the college. Mildred Brewster, 20, had had a physical relationship with Jack earlier. There was even some evidence when the case went to trial that indicated she may have been pregnant and had a home abortion. On May 29th, 1897, Mildred first went to the fields behind the college and took one practice shot with a gun she had purchased the week before. People confirmed they had heard a gunshot early in the morning. At 7 am, Mildred ended up at Anna's front door on Liberty Street, wanting to discuss their mutual connection to Jack, with a witness hearing Mildred say, "He can't be engaged to both of us. We will have to let him decide."

Then the two young women started to walk in the rain, under one umbrella, over to Jack's house. But as they approached, cutting through a meadow path that brought them in sight of his house, Mildred turned the gun on Anna and shot her through the head, and then turned the gun on herself.

Neighbors came out, including Jack, to try to help the two while they waited for doctors. Anna died of her injury, but Mildred survived. Her wealthy father hired skilled lawyers who successfully pled insanity, becoming the first time that tactic was used and setting a precedent for a defense we know well today. Mildred ended up spending most of the rest of her life in the Waterbury Hospital for the Insane (which later became a Vermont State

Employee Complex, and let me tell you, the boarded-up concrete rooms in the basement are really creepy).

Chapter Review

- Black Agnes, a large, distinctive monument depicting Death in Green Mount Cemetery, is said to curse those who sit on the tomb at night.

- Little Margaret, on the other hand, grants wishes to those who leave pennies or buttons at her gravestone in Green Mount Cemetery.

- Vermont College is haunted by the ghost of a murdered young woman who was killed by her fiancé's ex-lover.

Chapter 11: Beautiful and Historic Local Buildings

11.1 Overview

Montpelier tells the story of its history through many of its buildings and architecture. Prominent buildings throughout town feature an assortment of design choices based on trends at the time, such as Gothic revival, Queen Anne, Italianate, Second Empire, and Romanesque. Stone masonry and mid-century brick replaced the wooden buildings of the growing town after two city-wide fires. Some buildings were even put on train tracks in the 1800s and early 1900s and moved around State Street, like in a game of SimCity. Here are a few interesting chapters of Montpelier, as told through the town's structures.

11.2 Buildings Downtown

11.2.1 The Statehouse

The Statehouse, of course, is the reason you came to Montpelier, I'm sure. Montpelier was designated the Capital of Vermont not because it was a bustling, large town that would naturally be an epicenter for business and politics but because Montpelier was willing to quickly build a State House and lodge politicians in the local Pavilion hotel. This is our third one because that first build was eventually deemed too small, and the second one burned down.

Tip 99: The statue that adorns the top of the building is Ceres, the goddess of agriculture.

Tip 100: Find the tunnel that runs underneath the State House.

The tunnel starts from the Superior Court House and ends at the Tax Building. It is open to the public. The Statehouse itself is also open to the public.

Tip 101: Self-guided tours are available year-round.

The Main Lobby and the Sergeant-at-Arms' office offer free, informative maps and audio tour wands that you can check out. You can also listen to the audio tour on your phone by calling 802-526-3221 or scanning a QR code.

Tip 102: Free, guided tours are available.

These tours leave every half-hour from the Main Lobby and are available from late June through October, Monday-Friday, from 10:00 am to 3:30 pm, and Saturdays from 11:00 am-2:30 pm. At other times of the year, a guide must be arranged in advance by contacting the State House Tours Coordinator at visit@leg.state.vt.us or 802-461-9923.

Tip 103: You can sit in on our state legislative sessions.

If you'd like to see the legislature in action, visit in January through May. Visitors are allowed in the chambers and committee rooms as space permits. No reservations are necessary.

Tip 104: Have lunch at the State House.

Get shoulder-to-shoulder with our state legislators by having lunch with them at the State House cafeteria. Their menu offers decently priced breakfast and lunch options from 8:00 am-3:00 pm when the legislature is in session and 8:00 am-2:00 pm in the off-season.

11.2.2 The Tax Department

Originally, the imposing, granite-faced building to the left of the State House was home to National Life Insurance Company before they moved to their current location on a hill overlooking the town. You might also notice that the left side of the building is a dull, yellow brick façade and does not match the rest of the building. The original plan for this building was to expand a wing on that side of the building, which would have visually matched the rest of the exterior, but National Life moved before that plan was realized.

Tip 105: Check out the painted ceiling fresco in the main foyer of the Tax Department.

Before I learned about the Tax Building's former life as an insurance company, I thought it was so odd that such a serious-looking building and such a dreaded certainty of life that is often coupled with the term "death" would have such an ornate lobby. But if you venture into the building during usual business hours, you will be treated to an impressive fresco painted on the heavily vaulted ceiling.

11.2.3 The Pavilion

To the right of the State House sits the Pavilion. The original Pavilion was a hotel built in 1808. It was a very popular place to stay, not only for people out of town who were patients of the Keeley Institute being treated for addiction across the street but also for legislators coming from all over Vermont to work at the State House. By the mid-1900s, however, the hotel was falling into disuse, as the newer Tavern Hotel (now the Capital Plaza) had been built by then. As a result, the Pavilion Hotel was closed in 1966.

For the next few years, a battle raged between modern needs and historical value. The State of Vermont bought the failing building, eyeing the space as an excellent location for more government offices serving the Capital's needs. Local residents and historians fought the proposal of a modern-looking office building in their historic district, especially given the lengthy history of the Pavilion in town. The compromise was to demolish the old building, build a new steel and brick structure, and then make the front of the building look like the old hotel.

Tip 106: What you see as the front of the current building is the actual façade of the former building, which was saved before the rest of the structure was razed.

Today, the Pavilion houses the Vermont History Museum on the first floor, government offices, including the office of the Governor, and the Vermont Supreme Court.

Tip 107: The covered porch of the Pavilion is the best location for watching parades, rallies, or people.

11.2.4 The Secretary of State's Office Building

The Secretary of State's office across the street from the Pavilion was originally built to house the home office of Vermont Mutual Fire Insurance, and the second floor of which housed The Keeley Institute in the late 1800s, which was a franchise that specialized in treating addiction to alcohol with injections of bichloride of gold, or "the Keeley Cure." The men and women who attended the Institute often stayed at the Pavilion hotel and were allowed to enjoy the offerings of the growing town while they were being treated. Although the Keeley Institute claimed to cure alcoholics within four weeks with their treatment plans, the success rate was about the same as placebo models: 50%.

The roof is copper, which has a greenish patina from years of rain and oxidation. The bank next to it matches a lot of the same architectural features, and the roof design was built in the late 1990s.

11.2.5 City Hall

The steps as you walk up display a sign that says, "please do not sit here," and was put up when I was a teenager. One of the spots teens would gather was the steps of City Hall. Central location, sprawling steps, and far away from all of the schools, it was a natural choice for some angsty, pre-independents. However, as several editorials to the newspaper revealed, the older demographics of the city found the teens foreboding and were, therefore, hesitant to visit the public building to go to meetings, pay their taxes, or make sure their dog license was up to date. So a sign was erected, along with the handrails, to dissuade the youth from congregating there any further.

As you walk in the main entrance, you will see a large bell sitting prominently front-and-center in the lobby from the U.S.S. Montpelier. There is even a U.S.S. Montpelier Museum located off the Auditorium on the second floor, but you will need to get the key from the City Manager's Office.

Tip 108: City Hall has a wonderful collection of historical photographs displayed in the main hallways, showing small scenes from the budding capital city.

It always fascinates me to see pictures of horse-drawn carriages and dirt roads where there are now cars and parking spaces.

11.2.6 The Courthouse

The Washington County Courthouse is a striking building downtown, with its Roman columns and red façade. Atop the Courthouse sits a clock tower, which does not share the same architectural design. Originally, the Courthouse, constructed in 1844, had a different, smaller top on its roof that matched the style of the building. However, a fire in 1880 destroyed the tower, and at the time it was rebuilt French Second Empire design was in fashion, which is why it looks so similar to the tower at College Hall up the hill.

Tip 109: The Courthouse is a great place to sit and people-watch.

The Courthouse is located in a very central, heavily trafficked area (for Montpelier). Food stands are set up on the sidewalk outside the Courthouse in the summer, there is a little green space there to sit, and often there are benches under the apple trees so you can sit and watch small-town life go by.

11.2.7 The Old Jailhouse

Right behind the Courthouse is a smaller brick building with a hexagonal side tower facing Elm Street. This is the original jailhouse. Today, it houses the Washington County Sheriff's Department.

Fun fact: The jailhouse was originally built around the steel prisoner cells, which served as the internal, load-bearing structure of the building. When the jailhouse was renovated to provide more modern conditions and offices, the cells had to be carefully replaced with a new structure to keep the rest of the building from falling inwards.

11.2.8 The DMV Building

Completed in 1949, across the street from the State House lies a behemoth faced with all Vermont white marble, which, honestly, looks quite out of place with all the other historic buildings in the vicinity. When the design process started for this building in the 1930s, Modernistic style was the fashion, and less attention was paid at the time to incorporating its design with the current architectural examples on State Street. Even though most call it "the DMV building," it actually houses many other state government offices as well.

Details to note are the engraved names of all 14 of Vermont's counties across the top of the building, the figure of Ceres, the goddess of agriculture, and the man attaching a sap bucket to a maple tree carved in relief on the steel front door. If you enter the building, you can find a plaque that denotes the specific spot where famed Admiral George Dewey was born. His family home was moved, and two other historic family homes were demolished to provide space for this new state government building.

George Dewey is the only person in the United States to attain the rank of Admiral of the Navy. He was famous for his victory at Manila Bay during the Spanish-American War, where he annihilated the Spanish navy with only one American casualty.

11.2.9 The Department of Agriculture, Food, and Markets

Located at 116 State Street and built in the last decade of the 1800s, this building is a very unique structure. The architectural style is called Richardsonian Romanesque, which looks similar to its cousin, the Trinity Church in Copley Square, Boston. This was another location of the National Life Insurance Company headquarters. Its original interior was a fascinating mix of mahogany, Egyptian mosaic tiles on the floor, and warm shades of brown and tan marble. It also featured Vermont's very first elevator, which stayed in use until 1981, much to the terror of those who dared to use it.

11.2.10 The Dewey House

Edward Dewey's former home, designed by famed architect George Guernsey in the fashionable Queen Anne style, now rests at 128 State Street. Today used as a state government building; originally, this home resided at 120 State Street, the location of the current DMV building. Unfortunately, four homes of prominent Montpelier families had to be removed to make way for the new state office structure. Three of the homes were bought by the state under eminent domain and demolished, while the historical value of Edward Dewey's home was honored by putting the structure on railroad tracks and sending it down the street to its current location.

11.3 Churches

Given the small population of just over 7,000 people, and the secular leanings of Vermont in general, Montpelier's wide assortment of churches is sometimes a surprise.

11.3.1 St. Augustine Catholic Church

Originally built on Court Street, within the shadow of the Capitol Building, St. Augustine served Montpelier's small but growing population of Catholics, the majority of whom were French Canadians and Irish immigrant laborers. Between 1830 and 1892, the Catholic priests serving Montpelier would continually improve upon their parish until, in 1892, the first cornerstone was laid at St. Augustine's current site on Barre Street.

The impressive gothic structure you see today took 11 years to finish and was barely ready for their first celebration, Easter Mass, in 1903. This was a community project and a community celebration. Members of the parish helped install pews on the Holy Saturday, nuns decorated the building inside and out, and women of the parish brought the vestments and a lace alb for the priest. Many of the city's residents embraced this celebration, so many that the church had to distribute nearly 500 tickets to the three Easter masses for the non-Catholics in town. Despite the capacity for 900 seated in the pews, the first mass had close to 1400 in attendance.

While the building stands stoically, built of granite and brick and raised up from street level, the inside is full of stained-glass panels by famous artist Wilbur Herbert Burnham, dating back to the early 20th century. Valued today at half a million dollars, these panels tell the story of Jesus and bring rich, colorful light into the spacious, warm main hall.

Tip 110: Contact the Rectory at 802-223-5285 during weekday office hours to be let into the church to enjoy the interior.

11.3.2 Christ Episcopal Church

Located on State Street across from the Court House, Christ Episcopal Church is another example of gothic, granite architecture found in town. Originally built a little closer to the Capitol Building in 1840, it moved to its current location in 1868, using light granite exclusively from the neighboring towns of Barre and Berlin.

This is a church that continually meets structural damage with community support. In 1903, the roof was burned off completely, and the parish and community came together to rebuild. In 1927, the famous flood in Montpelier devastated the church, and yet again, the community came together to rebuild it, spending more on the reconstruction than the church had cost to build 60 years prior. The bell tower that stands used to have a steeple and spire rising 100 feet over the grounds, which had to be removed in 1963 to prevent accruing damage to the tower itself. Then in 2015, as the roof was being repaired and the capstones were being removed, the base pin of the crane being used failed and fell against the roof, creating additional damage. Again, the parish worked hard to raise funds with the community's help, and the roof was repaired.

Christ Church was where my mother went when she felt called back to the church, seeing its open doors on a spring day inviting her to come and sit and feel that connection again.

The courtyard adjacent to the church is regularly used by the community as a place to have lunch outside. During the summer, there are often mid-day live musicians who treat the public to performances of bluegrass, jazz, and folk music.

11.3.3 Bethany Church

Founded in 1808, this church is a local pioneer of social justice in the community. As stated in the mission:

"We are an Open and Affirming Congregation, we have publicly stated that LGBTQ people are welcome and affirm that they are fully a part of our life and leadership. Our members are extremely active in pursuit of peace and justice on the local, regional and international levels."

Alongside the church, they also support the Bethany Center for Spirituality through the Arts, which aims to encourage and enhance the spiritual health of the community through music and art.

The building stands as yet another example of gothic stonework and architecture and has undergone some transformations over its time situated on Main Street. Originally much more ornate, the sanctuary of the building was demolished in 1954 as parts of the stone structure started to fall off. A more modern building was then built, using stones from the original structure to help blend its new look with the older steeple and chapel.

11.3.4 The Unitarian Church of Montpelier

Across from the Kellogg-Hubbard Library and diagonal from Bethany Church sits the stately, classic New England-style white façade Unitarian Church. Another example of a progressive pastoral response to changing times, the Unitarian Church of Montpelier was the first church in the city to perform a civil union ceremony when civil unions became recognized under Vermont law in 2000.

Designed by the same architect as the State House building, Thomas Silloway, the Renaissance Revival-style church (then known as the Church of the Messiah) was dedicated in 1866. However, the belfry he designed for the church remained without a bell until 1983. Today, children ring the bell every Sunday, calling congregants to the morning service.

This stately building survived the floods of 1927 and 1992, repairing the damages each time and welcoming parishioners back to worship.

Tip 111: Inside, the sage-green paint choices were approved by the Montpelier Design Review Committee, not the church itself, in 2012.

For 80 years, the church had struck an all-white aesthetic, inside and out. The choice of a green accent color for this historic building required town approval and, once approved, paved the way to have the same accent color represented on the steeple.

In 2013, the Unitarian Church of Montpelier was designated as a "Welcoming Congregation" by the Unitarian Universalist Association, which recognized the church's work and ongoing commitment to welcoming members of the LGBTQ+ community.

11.3.5 Trinity Methodist Church

On the other side of the Kellogg-Hubbard Library from the Bethany Church is the Trinity Methodist Church, built in 1874, 70 years after Montpelier was first designated as part of the "Barre Circuit" of Methodists in the area. At the time, Montpelier only had 6-8 Methodist residents. By 1838, there were 99 congregants in Montpelier who worshipped at a meeting house on what is now Court Street. The current church structure has been the home of Trinity Methodist for almost 150 years.

11.4 Private Homes

11.4.1 The Old Arsenal

At the corner of College and Arsenal Street is a small brick cottage that looks nothing like its neighbors. Flanked by Victorian- and

Colonial-style homes, this tiny house, by comparison, is set back more from the road and does not draw attention to itself.

This home is the last of three brick buildings that comprised Montpelier's Civil War arsenal and document storage, at the time conveniently located down the street from the US Army's Sloan General Hospital, where Vermont College now resides.

Originally, there were two other brick buildings, one much larger in the middle of two smaller structures. However, in 1945, a fire caused by lightning destroyed the other two buildings, and the remnants were razed so the land could be divided into residential lots. The small brick arsenal building remains now as a private residence, reminding us of our Civil War history.

11.4.2 Redstone Mansion

Now tucked away, barely noticeable from Terrace Street, lies a grand, red sandstone and brick mansion that used to be the most prominent private residence in Montpelier. It was built for the Burgess family by George Guernsey in 1891, a famous local architect who also designed the St. Augustine Roman Catholic Church and the French and Blanchard blocks downtown.

Blending the styles of the Bavarian hunting lodge, Queen Anne, and Romanesque, it features a wrap-around porch, a conical tower, asymmetrical roofs, wood paneling and floors inside, and ornate fireplaces and windows.

Bought by the State of Vermont, it formerly housed the Vermont State Police and then the Secretary of State's Office. Finally, it was used for displaced state employees when Hurricane Irene ravaged the Waterbury State Complex. Finally, the home was put up for private sale when it was clear the cost of upkeep was no longer financially viable for the state.

The main driveway is now chained off, although no one seems to know who the new residents are or if the buyers are even currently living there. Sometimes there is a car parked near the house, but there is no known activity at or around the house. Before the chain went up, my friends and I would walk the driveway and then passed the house, where a stone stairway leads into a little forested glade near a stream. You can imagine what an amazing sight this house once was when it could be seen; however, now the woods are overgrown around it, and the house remains largely hidden from view.

11.4.3 The Gingerbread House

Originally called Athenwood, the summer home of famous artist Thomas Waterman Wood (of The Wood Gallery fame), this funky house rests on the side of a ledge as you travel up Northfield Street, away from the city center. As of writing this, it is painted tan, but when I was a kid, it was dark brownish-red. Covered in ornate carvings along the eaves, thin, tall stained-glass windows, and peaked roofs, we all thought it was a witch's house, straight out of Hansel and Gretel.

Next door, with some resemblance to Athenwood, is Wood's studio which was built after the main home. Both are private residences now.

Chapter Review

- Visit the Statehouse to enjoy the interior art and architecture of the smallest capital in the United States.

- There is a tunnel running under the State House that starts at the Tax Department and ends at the Vermont Supreme Court building.

- Make sure to walk into the Tax Department on State Street (only open during the week) to see the fresco and ornate interior architecture.

- The Pavilion used to be a hotel catering to lawmakers and guests visiting the Keeley Institute across the street to address addiction. The front of the building you see is just the literal façade of the previous building, pasted onto a newer structure.

- The five major examples of local church architecture are found within a square mile of each other, all in downtown Montpelier, three of which are triangulated around the Kellogg-Hubbard Library.

- One of the few remaining structures from the Civil War, the small brick Arsenal home is tucked away on College Street.

- Thomas W. Wood's summer home and studio look like gingerbread houses or witches' houses, depending on who you ask. A rare architectural find.

Frequently Asked Questions

Is Montpelier named after Montpellier, France?

Yes. The first permanent settlement in Montpelier, constructed in 1787 by Colonel Jacob Davis, apparently gave him the right to name the charted land. France was very popular with Americans at the time since they had supported the American colonies during the Revolutionary War, so Davis chose a French town to name the new settlement after.

This method of paying homage to another country by naming a town after them is fairly common all along the East Coast and especially in New England but is not quite as dramatic as our neighbor, Barre, whose name was purportedly chosen by the winner of a wrestling match.

Can I ride my bike/scooter/skateboard on the sidewalks? What about my kids?

Yes and No. Montpelier actually had quite a lively debate about this on Front Porch Forum (a town-specific newsletter/forum posted 1-2 times a day). The final conclusion is this: If there are metered parking spaces along the street, you should be riding on the road, not on the sidewalk. Wherever there are no meters, it's expected that you move aside or into the road from the sidewalk whenever there are pedestrians. It is called a SideWALK, after all. It's made for them. If you have small children and are worried about using the bike lanes in town, there is some forgiveness for kids riding on the sidewalk *as long as* there are not a lot of pedestrians. Pedestrians have the right of way.

Although I did have one man in a car nearly sideswipe my daughter and me, causing her to fall into the road, so he could tell me we shouldn't be riding on the sidewalk (where there was no one walking and no meters and I was trying to show my daughter how she could get to town on her own.) So, idiots and jerks are still around to tell you what they think of your decisions. Still, after the town populace agreed on these general sidewalk rules and etiquette,

I would be willing to tell anyone where they can go with their poor driving and lack of awareness.

Does Bernie Sanders live here?

No, Bernie does not live in Montpelier, but he does often make an appearance in the July 3rd parade.

What is that awful noise I hear at night sometimes that sounds like an animal dying?

That is probably a fisher, sometimes called a fisher cat, which actually looks more like a big weasel than a cat. It sounds like death. A local resident told me there are some that hunt in the fields behind Vermont College and sometimes can be heard in the sewers in the neighborhood. (Thank you, Kim!)

Other wildlife that sound concerning: foxes and coyotes. Foxes are more screechy than you would expect but not as death-is-imminent as fishers. Coyotes have that classic howl. You might not hear them as much downtown, but if you get an Airbnb closer to the country, you might hear them howl. Very "Wild Kingdom" out here.

What is some of the lingo I should know about?

If you hear a Vermonter, you will probably notice a few things that are different pronunciations or vocabulary than what you're used to. For example, I know when I moved to Virginia for college, all my new friends noted that I spoke like a "Yankee," so apparently, this is a thing. I thought I sounded like them, but apparently, I did not.

First off, the "t" in "mountain" or "Vermont" is not pronounced. I don't know where it went, but it just falls off to the point that it's more like a guttural vowel sound than it is a consonant anymore. "Mountain" sounds like "moun- [sound that is no longer a "t"]-in." "Vermont" sounds like "Vermon [hard stop like you were going to continue with a "t," but then you opted out]." If we dared to say "soft-serve," it would sound more like "sof-serve," and we would still make a face that we were not saying "creemee."

We call it "soda," not "pop."

We call it a "sub," not a "hoagie."

The "er" in just about any word has a bit more push to it than you might be used to. A real, backwoods Vermonter can make this sound through his teeth, almost like a growl.

We use "wicked" to mean "really." Example: "It's snowing wicked hard out there."

"Flatlanders" are people who are not from a mountainous state. We might accept New Hampshire or Maine into our ranks, but New Jersey? You are a flatlander. I've been to New Jersey. No mountains. Very flat.

Why is distance measured in time and not miles?

This is such a fun question because when you live here, this makes so much sense.

If we lived in a place with real straight roads and very predictable, mild weather, we too might measure distance with real distance measurements. But here's the reality: most of the roads you take are not straight, some are made of dirt, sometimes weather prevents you from going the speed limit, and sometimes the fastest way to get somewhere is very windy and convoluted. So your destination might literally be 20 miles in a straight line, but the driving distance could be much longer, also depending on the route you choose to take.

So I think Vermont just gave up trying to give useless information such as distance when the more important information is how long it is going to take you to get there. I mean, really, how long travel takes is what we all grapple with. If driving somewhere took five minutes or five hours, that's all I'd want to know. How long am I going to be in the car? So we cut to the chase and just tell you that.

Barre, VT, is about 10-15 minutes away, longer if it's snowing.

Burlington is about 45 minutes away by highway, 50-55 minutes away if you take the local roads, and a full hour or more if it's bad weather.

Stowe is about a half hour away, but if you're going to Stowe Mountain, it's more like 45 minutes, and if it's tourist season, you're going to be stuck in your car for at least an hour because there is one road in, and one road out, and everyone is on it.

See? Distance doesn't matter to you. Time does.

Thanks for giving me that Cliff Street spot to photograph Montpelier. Are there any other locations for spectacular views?

Why, yes!

Not really within walking distance, but another prime location to get beautiful pictures of Vermont, Gould Hill is a "top of the world" type spot in the open countryside with panoramic views of mountains, fields, and farms.

To get there, take North Street off Main Street (right beside Main Street Middle School) and just drive. North Street can get steep and narrow at times and eventually turns to dirt, so drive carefully and enjoy the cool houses built up along the way, especially as you get further away from town. When the road finally plateaus, you will be reaching the top of Gould Hill, and I'll assume you can see for yourself all the beauty that surrounds you.

If you're like me and do not like to backtrack, after you take your pictures and consider how realistic it might be to build a home out here, continue down the road until there is a road veering to the left. This road will take you past several working farms, maybe some cows, all the way down back to the pavement. When you hit the main paved road, you will be on Elm Street, way past the Rec Fields and the North Branch Nature Center, so make a left and head back to town!

About the Author

Jody Andreoletti lives in a wooded neighborhood in Montpelier, Vermont, with her two daughters and her best friend from childhood. Living here for almost 40 years, she grew up in the capital of Vermont, leaving for college in Virginia and some grad school in Boston, Massachusetts. In 2002, Jody returned to Vermont to enjoy the neighborly community the state offers and be closer to nature. After obtaining her Master's degree from Norwich University, she worked in information security and instructional technology until her second daughter was born. When she is not writing or editing, Jody is a foodie who loves to travel and learn new languages, is an avid gardener, and trains and instructs in Brazilian Jiu-Jitsu.

HowExpert publishes quick how to guides on all topics from A to Z by everyday experts. Visit HowExpert.com to learn more.

About the Publisher

Byungjoon "BJ" Min is an author, publisher, entrepreneur, and the founder of HowExpert. He started off as a once broke convenience store clerk to eventually becoming a fulltime internet marketer and finding his niche in publishing. He is the founder and publisher of HowExpert where the mission is to discover, empower, and maximize everyday people's talents to ultimately make a positive impact in the world for all topics from A to Z. Visit BJMin.com and HowExpert.com to learn more. John 14:6

Recommended Resources

- HowExpert.com – How To Guides on All Topics from A to Z by Everyday Experts.
- HowExpert.com/free – Free HowExpert Email Newsletter.
- HowExpert.com/books – HowExpert Books
- HowExpert.com/courses – HowExpert Courses
- HowExpert.com/clothing – HowExpert Clothing
- HowExpert.com/membership – HowExpert Membership Site
- HowExpert.com/affiliates – HowExpert Affiliate Program
- HowExpert.com/jobs – HowExpert Jobs
- HowExpert.com/writers – Write About Your #1 Passion/Knowledge/Expertise & Become a HowExpert Author.
- HowExpert.com/resources – Additional HowExpert Recommended Resources
- YouTube.com/HowExpert – Subscribe to HowExpert YouTube.
- Instagram.com/HowExpert – Follow HowExpert on Instagram.
- Facebook.com/HowExpert – Follow HowExpert on Facebook.
- TikTok.com/@HowExpert – Follow HowExpert on TikTok.

Made in the USA
Middletown, DE
13 August 2023

36643141R00076